MUFFINS
GALORE

CATHERINE ATKINSON

Published by MQ Publications Limited

12 The Ivories, 6–8 Northampton Street

London N1 2HY

Tel: 44 (0)20 7359 2244

Fax: 44 (0)20 7359 1616

email: mail@mqpublications.com

North American office

49 West 24th Street

New York, NY 10010

Email: information@mqpublicationsus.com

£157,007

Website: www.mqpublications.com

Copyright © MQ Publications Limited 2006

PHOTOGRAPHY: Marie Louise Avery

HOME ECONOMIST: Kim Morphew

STYLIST: Rachel Jukes

RECIPE CREDITS: see page 192

ISBN 10: 1-84601-111-6

ISBN 13: 978-1-84601-111-5

1 3 5 7 9 0 8 6 4 2

Printed and bound in China

This book contains the opinions and ideas of the author. It is intended to provide helpful and informative material on the subjects addressed in this book and is sold with the understanding that the author and publisher are not engaged in rendering any kind of personal professional services in this book. The author and publisher disclaim all responsibility for any liability, loss or risk, personal or otherwise, which is incurred as a consequence, directly or indirectly, of the use and application of any of the contents of this book.

CONTENTS

INTRODUCTION

When it comes to a quick-and-easy treat, nothing beats freshly baked, mouthwatering muffins. This fabulous recipe collection has more than 100 flavour combinations for every occasion, from sweet and sticky muffins to savoury and healthy, wholesome varieties.

★ AN AMERICAN INVENTION ★

The name 'muffin' is given to two very different types of bakes: one, the yeast-leavened English muffin, was known as far back as the 11th century. This thick, flat bun is served split and toasted and lavishly buttered as a traditional English tea-time bake, although the name comes from the French 'moufflet', meaning a soft bread. The other, an American invention, began as a yeast bread, but gradually evolved to be a 'quick bread' (that is, a dough risen chemically using a raising agent rather than yeast). Quite distinguishable from its English counterpart, it's this type of muffin that features in this book.

★ EARLY MUFFINS ★

The true tale of the American muffin remains a bit of a mystery, as recipes were kept a secret within families and small communities. They were, however, featured in cookery books at the end of the 18th century when 'pearl ash' (potassium carbonate) was discovered in America. This was a refined form of potash, which produced carbon dioxide when mixed with an acid and a liquid, or an acidic liquid such as soured milk. Housewives no longer needed to wait for the action of yeast to rise their baked goods. Made quickly and simply, muffins were first served as a hot breakfast food. Gradually different kinds of grains were used, such as corn, wheat and oatmeal, and a small range of flavours created with berries, apples, raisins and nuts.

Early versions were much less sweet than contemporary ones and remained very bread-like with little fat. This was mainly because pearl ash produced a soapy taste when combined with butter or lard, so only very small quantities of these could be added to the mixture if the muffin was to remain edible!

This changed when a few decades later sodium bicarbonate – now known as bicarbonate of soda – was used to make muffins. It worked in exactly the same way as pearl ash, in the presence of an acid and a liquid, but with no soapy aftertaste. A few years later, when baking powder was created, muffins could be made without an acid; flavours such as chocolate and coffee began to be used in muffins. At first muffins were baked in 'gem irons' – ridged lozenge-shaped pans. With the invention of paper muffin cups, these difficult-to-clean pans quickly lost popularity and circular-shaped muffins became the norm. In the 1950s, packaged muffin mixes became available in the supermarkets and the popularity and variety of muffins grew at a rapid rate. A decade later, they were in such demand that chains of coffee shop-style muffin eateries started appearing both in America and throughout the world.

★ MUFFIN-MAKING TODAY ★

In more recent years, there has been a resurgence in home-baking as many consumers have turned away from commercially produced products packed with artificial additives. No shop-bought muffin can match one that is made from fresh ingredients and the pleasure that home-baking provides. For today's busy cook, whether a novice or experienced, muffins are the perfect bake, which can be mixed and cooked in minutes. Nowadays, the range of ingredients is vast and so are the possible combinations. The only limitation in muffin-making is your imagination.

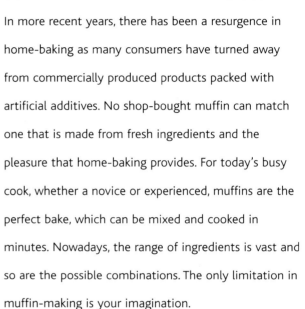

EQUIPMENT

Unlike cakes and cookies, very few specialist items are needed for muffins; they can be made with nothing more sophisticated than a set of weighing scales or calibrated measuring cups, a mixing bowl and spoon and a muffin tin or a few paper muffin cups on a baking tray. However, using the right equipment will simplify muffin-making and ensure success every time.

★ MEASURES ★

Accurate weighing scales or calibrated measuring cups are essential when making muffins. You also need a set of measuring spoons, particularly when adding baking powder and bicarbonate of soda. For measuring liquid, use a clearly calibrated measuring jug, in glass, plastic or stainless steel.

★ BOWLS ★

Whether you choose a glass, ceramic or stainless-steel bowl, make sure that it is large enough to contain both the dry and wet ingredients and with enough room for easy mixing. A deep bowl is preferable to a wide, shallow one. In addition, small heat-proof bowls are useful for melting butter or chocolate and for beating eggs.

★ SIFTER ★

In most muffin recipes, it is unnecessary to sift the dry ingredients. A sifter is useful, however, for making frostings for topping muffins and for dusting icing sugar or cocoa powder over baked muffins. You can also buy dredgers with tiny holes or a very fine mesh for this purpose.

★ TIMER ★

This is essential as a few extra minutes in the oven can result in overcooked, dry muffins. Many modern ovens are fitted with a timer; if not, a digital timer or one with a rotating dial and a loud ring is a good investment.

★ WIRE RACK ★

After baking, muffins should be transferred to a wire rack, even if you are planning to serve them warm. The rack will allow air to circulate under the muffins and prevent them going soggy.

★ SPATULA ★

A flexible plastic or rubber spatula can be used to scrape the last little bit of muffin mixture from the bowl. It can also be used to fold the dry and wet ingredients together.

★ MUFFIN TINS ★

These vary greatly in quality and if you're a keen muffin-maker, it's worth buying a heavyweight muffin tin that will absorb and hold heat, helping your muffins rise higher and have a better colour. A non-stick one is preferable as some types of muffins are better made directly in the tin rather than in paper cups. Muffin tins come in a variety of sizes, but the standard muffin tin has 12 cups, each about 7cm in diameter and 3cm deep. Mini muffin tins are also popular; again they have 12 holes, but these are a dainty 4cm in diameter and 2cm deep. The new non-stick silicone muffin moulds are very handy as they can be used at high temperatures without any additional preparation. They are extremely easy to clean and in some types the material bends allowing the muffins to pop out easily. You do, however, need to place a baking sheet under the non-rigid ones.

★ PAPER MUFFIN CASES ★

You can lightly grease muffin tins, but for ease, paper muffin cups make a great alternative. Not only do they save time and washing up, but they also help keep muffins fresh and make packing muffins for cold lunches and picnics a doddle. Plain pleated white paper cups are the most economical, but there is also a huge range of fancy designs for every occasion available at supermarkets and cake decorating shops.

★ PIPING BAGS AND NOZZLES ★

These are useful for piping whipped cream, frostings, icing and melted chocolate when decorating cooled muffins. Most piping bags are now made of nylon; the best are glued and double stitched along the seams to prevent splitting or leakage. You can also buy disposable plastic piping bags, or make your own from greaseproof paper or baking parchment.

★ PASTRY BRUSHES ★

While it's easy to drizzle sticky glazes such as honey, maple syrup and hot sugar syrups over muffins with a teaspoon, a pastry brush will give an all-over, even finish. Choose a brush with either natural bristles fixed in a wooden handle or one with nylon bristles and a plastic handle. After use, rinse in cold water, then wash in hot soapy water, flick dry and leave to air before using again.

★ AIRTIGHT CONTAINERS ★

Most muffins keep well if stored in an airtight plastic container or tin in a cool place. A large shallow one, which will hold the muffins in a single layer is preferable. As a general guide, muffins will keep for around 3–5 days.

★ PLASTIC FREEZER BAGS ★

All of the muffins in this book can be frozen prior to being iced or decorated, unless otherwise indicated and the easiest way to do this is in re-sealable plastic freezer bags, clearly marked with the date the muffins were made. Muffins can be kept frozen for up to 3 months.

INGREDIENTS

Good-quality ingredients are at the heart of successful muffin-making, as muffins are made from only a few basics — butter or oil, sugar, flour, eggs and flavourings.

★ FLOUR ★

Muffins are made with either ordinary plain or self-raising flour, as these have low gluten content, resulting in a soft, cake-like texture. Self-raising flour contains raising agents, but often extra baking powder and/or bicarbonate of soda is added as well to make the muffins really light. Always check the 'use-by' date as raising agents gradually deteriorate. If you want to substitute plain flour for self-raising in a recipe, you will need to add 1 teaspoon for every 100g of flour. Wholemeal flour is milled from the whole wheat kernel and is coarser in texture, giving a heavier result, so is often combined with plain flour.

★ NON WHEAT FLOUR ★

Cornmeal, also known as polenta or maizemeal, has tiny bright yellow grains and is particularly good in savoury muffins. Use medium-ground cornmeal, unless the recipe states otherwise.

Cornflour is a fine white powder made from cornmeal. Used in small quantities in muffins combined with flour, it gives a lighter, smooth texture.

Soya flour is made by grinding soya beans to a powder. It has a distinctive nutty taste and is useful for making gluten-free muffins.

Rice flour, produced by finely grinding white or brown rice is again useful in gluten-free cooking. It gives muffins a light, slightly crumbly texture.

★ RAISING AGENTS ★

Raising agents react in contact with water and produce carbon dioxide bubbles, so it is essential to bake muffins as soon as they have been mixed. Baking powder is a mixture of alkaline bicarbonate of soda and an acid such as cream of tartar. Bicarbonate of soda needs an acid ingredient as well as liquid in order to work, so is often used in citrus-based muffins and those with buttermilk or yoghurt. Store raising agents in a dry place and use within their 'use-by' date as they deteriorate when kept.

★ BUTTER ★

Butter keeps muffins moist and adds a distinct flavour and colour. When making muffins with melted butter, cut it into small pieces, so that it melts quickly, and place in a saucepan (or microwave in a bowl) over a low heat to prevent it burning. Remove it from the heat when it has almost melted and allow the residual heat to finish the job.

For rubbed-in muffin mixtures, remove the butter from the fridge about 10 minutes before using, so that it is still cold but not too hard. For creamed mixtures, let the butter come to room temperature, so that it is soft and easy to beat. If you use butter to grease muffin pans, choose unsalted, as salted butter may make the muffin edges stick. Block margarine may be used as an alternative to butter for muffins. It won't produce quite the same flavour as butter, but is usually less expensive.

★ OIL ★

Oil is sometimes used in muffins instead of solid fat. It's especially good in quick-mix muffins because, unlike butter, it doesn't need to be melted and cooled first.

★ SUGAR ★

Sugar is essential in many muffin recipes, including savoury ones, to achieve a good texture, but the quality can usually be increased or decreased slightly to suit personal taste. There are many different types of sugar, each with different characteristics.

Caster sugar is the most frequently used in muffin-making, as it has a fine grain, which combines well with other ingredients. Golden caster sugar, the unrefined version, is a pale gold colour.

Granulated sugar has large granules and is used for crunchy toppings and sometimes in rubbed-in mixtures.

Demerara is a deep golden colour with a toffee-like flavour and even larger granules. It's particularly good for sprinkling over the tops of muffins before baking.

Soft light and dark brown sugar are refined white sugars that have been tossed in syrup or molasses to darken the colour and to flavour them. Soft brown sugar makes moister muffins than caster sugar, so if you substitute one for the other, add a tiny bit less or more liquid to compensate.

Muscovado sugar is unrefined and made from raw sugar cane. It is a very moist brown sugar that has a treacly flavour and tends to be slightly less sweet than refined sugars.

Icing sugar is ground to a fine powder. It is rarely used in muffin mixtures, but makes smooth icings and frostings and may be dusted over the tops of muffins for an easy, professional finish.

Other sweeteners may be used in muffins, including golden syrup, maple syrup and honey.

★ EGGS ★

Most of the recipes in this book use medium eggs, unless stated otherwise. Always use eggs at room temperature as cold eggs may curdle and cold egg whites will produce less volume when whisked.

★ FRUIT & NUTS ★

Dried and candied fruit, including apples, apricots, tropical fruits, sour cherries, cranberries and blueberries and small whole or chopped nuts may be added to your favourite muffin mix without altering the consistency of the batter. If you want to add fresh fruit, it is better to use a recipe written for this, as the additional moisture will affect the final result.

★ CHOCOLATE ★

Chocolate muffins may be made either with cocoa powder or by stirring melted or chopped chocolate into the batter. Chocolate chips or dots are a quick way to add chocolate flavour and come in milk, white and plain varieties. For the very best flavour, use plain chocolate with at least 70% cocoa solids.

★ SPICES & FLAVOURINGS ★

These are a great way to add flavour to muffins, and warm spices, such as cinnamon and ginger, work particularly well in sweet muffins. Vanilla is probably the most frequently added spice and provides a delicate, subtle flavour. Choose pure vanilla extract if you can. Other useful muffin flavourings are grated citrus zest – use unwaxed fruit if possible – and salt, which helps bring out the flavour in both sweet and savoury muffins. If you prefer, you can use a low-sodium substitute.

SEVEN STEPS TO
successful muffin-making

Muffins are quick and easy to make, but there is some basic know-how that will make them even easier. Follow these seven simple steps and every batch you bake will be perfect.

★ NO.1 – PREPARING TINS ★

Spread an even layer of vegetable oil or melted unsalted butter or white vegetable margarine on the bottom and sides of each cup with a pastry brush or kitchen paper. Do not use too much, however, or the muffins will fry instead of bake. Pleated paper cups provide an easy alternative to greasing the pans.

★ NO.2 – MAKING THE MIXTURE ★

Always measure ingredients, particularly flour and liquid, very carefully. There are two ways of making muffins. The most popular is known in culinary terms as 'the muffin method'. This is the classic way; quick and easy. To get the right consistency, start by thoroughly combining the dry ingredients in a large mixing bowl and making a well in the middle. Combine the liquid ingredients, then pour them into the well. Use a rubber spatula or spoon to gently combine and moisten the dry ingredients. Stop mixing while the batter is still lumpy; the lumps will disappear when the muffins are baked.

The second is referred to as 'the creaming method'. This is slightly more time-consuming and produces cake-like muffins. This can also be divided into seven steps:

1. Preheat the oven and prepare the muffin pans.

2. Cream the butter until really light and fluffy.

3. Add the eggs, one at a time, beating well after each addition.

4. Combine the dry ingredients in a separate bowl to evenly distribute the leavening.

5. Gradually add the dry ingredients to the egg mixture, alternating with any liquid and flavourings.

6. Stir the batter until it is just combined; it should still have a few lumps in it.

7. Spoon the batter into the muffin pans or cups, add any topping and and bake straight away.

★ NO.3 – ADDING EXTRA INGREDIENTS ★

Stir ingredients such as dried fruit, nuts and chocolate chips into the dry ingredients before liquid is added. Moist and soft ingredients such as berries should be added when the batter is half-mixed to avoid crushing them. Gently fold them in, using a down, up and over motion, to ensure that they are distributed evenly through the mixture.

£151,00 7

★ NO.4 – FILLING THE TINS ★

Once the batter is mixed, the baking agent has been activated, so you need to get the muffins into the oven as soon as possible; the tins should already be greased or lined with paper cups and any toppings should be prepared. Scoop up the batter with a large spoon and push it off the spoon into the prepared tins using another spoon. Fill standard cups about two-thirds full and mini muffin tins just a little higher. If you want really large, mushroom-shaped muffins, fill the cups almost to the rim, but grease the entire top of the muffin tin first, to prevent the tops of the muffins from sticking to the area around each cup.

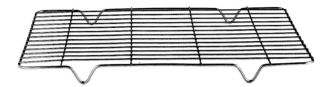

★ NO.5 – BAKING ★

It's essential to preheat the oven before you start mixing your muffins. Bake the muffins as soon as you've filled the tins, on the middle oven shelf or just a little higher. Close the oven door as quickly as possible to prevent heat being lost. Cook the muffins for a minute less than the recommended cooking time and check to see if they are done (if you have a clear glass oven door, you can do this without opening the oven). Remove them when they are just ready, as they will continue cooking in the residual heat of the tin.

★ NO.6 – REMOVING FROM THE PAN ★

As soon as you remove the muffins from the oven, place the tin on a wire cooling rack, then leave the muffins to stand for 4–5 minutes or for the time recommended in the recipe (moist muffins such as chocolate ones may need longer to firm up). Don't leave muffins in the tin for longer than 10 minutes, or they may be difficult to remove. Carefully loosen muffins from the tin by running a small spatula around the side, then lift out and place on the wire rack to prevent the bottoms going soggy.

★ NO.7 – STORING ★

Many muffins are best served and eaten warm; others are equally good when cold. Because home-made muffins do not contain preservatives, they should be stored in an airtight contain as soon as they are cool. They are best eaten fresh on the day of making, but most will keep well for 3–4 days. Keep those covered with a butter-based icing, or that contain ingredients such as fresh fruit, cheese or ham, in the fridge. Muffins can also be frozen for up to 3 months and will take about 30 minutes to thaw at room temperature or just a few seconds in the microwave.

★ TOPPING IDEAS ★

A tasty topping adds the final flourish to muffins and can turn an ordinary bake into a really special treat. It can range from a simple sprinkling of sugar or nuts, to brushing with a shiny glaze or a swirl of colourful frosting. Where quantities of ingredients are given, there is sufficient to top 10–12 standard-size muffins.

TOPPINGS TO ADD BEFORE BAKING:

★ A crunchy sugar topping is easy and effective. Use coarse sugars such as granulated, demerara or irregular-shaped amber sugar crystals or crushed sugar lumps.

★ Chopped and flaked nuts can be sprinkled over muffins in the same way as sugar. Nuts brown during baking, so check towards the end of cooking time. If they have browned sufficiently, but the muffins aren't quite cooked, put a baking tray on the shelf above the muffins; this will help stop the nuts from browning further, while the muffins finish cooking.

★ Candy-coated chocolate buttons retain their bright colours when baked, so look good scattered over the tops of muffins.

★ For a streusel topping, ideal for fruit muffins, rub 40g cold cubed butter into 50g plain flour until the mixture resembles breadcrumbs. Stir in 2 tablespoons caster or soft light brown sugar, then gently squeeze into a ball. Wrap and chill for 15 minutes, then coarsely grate before sprinkling over the muffin batter.

★ For a crumble topping, make in the same way as streusel topping but don't squeeze the dough together. Try adding other flavourings such as a pinch of ground cinnamon, chopped nuts or porridge oats.

★ To give savoury muffins an attractive finish, sprinkle them with a few sunflower seeds, poppy seeds, sesame seeds, porridge oats or finely grated Parmesan.

★ For a savoury crumble topping, rub 25g butter into 40g plain flour, then stir in 25g grated Cheddar cheese.

TROUBLESHOOTING

Occasionally muffins don't turn out quite as you had hoped. Try to work out what went wrong and why, so you can avoid the same problem when you bake the next batch.

Q – *Although they look perfect on the outside, my muffins have 'tunnels' of air in them when broken open. How can I avoid this?*

A – Quite simply, you're over-mixing the batter. Tunnels are caused by an excess of air bubbles in the mixture. Excessive stirring also develops the gluten in the flour, so the muffins will be tough. Next time, gently stir the dry and wet ingredients together until they are just combined. Stop mixing while the batter is still a bit lumpy.

Q – *Unfortunately I can't eat butter and would like to make muffins with oil instead. Is this possible?*

A – Yes, butter and oil are interchangeable in most recipes. Remember, though, that butter contains only about 80% fat, the other 20% being milk solids and water, so reduce the amount of oil very slightly and make up to the same amount with a dash of milk or water, e.g. if a recipe calls for 8 tablespoons of butter, use 7 tablespoons of oil and 1 tablespoon of milk or water. When choosing oil, sunflower or safflower oils are preferable for sweet muffins because they have a mild flavour, while for muffins containing nuts, groundnut oil works well. The more distinctive flavour of olive oil is good for many savoury muffin recipes.

Q – *Some recipes only make 9 or 10 muffins. I find my muffin tin warps when I don't fill all 12 cups with mixture, making them rise unevenly. What can I do?*

A – Even good-quality, heavy-weight muffin tins warp sometimes. You can prevent this happening by pouring some hot water into any empty muffin cups before baking – they should be about one-third full. The steam will help the muffins to rise as well.

Q – *My last batch of muffins were dry and tough. What did I do wrong?*

A – There are a couple of reasons why this may have happened. Firstly, when making muffins, the ratio of flour to liquid is vital, so always measure these carefully. If you use cup measures, take care not to pack down the flour tightly, and scrape off the excess with the flat blade of a knife to ensure it's completely level. Another cause of tough, dry muffins is over-baking; they are ready as soon as the tops spring back when lightly pressed with a finger, or when a cocktail stick inserted into the middle comes out clean.

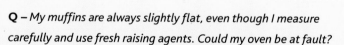

Q – *I'd like to make mini muffins instead of standard-sized ones from my favourite recipe. Is this possible?*

A – Most muffin recipes can be made into the muffin size of your choice. Generally speaking, you can make 3 mini muffins to every 1 standard size muffin. A mini-muffin pan holds about 2 tablespoons of batter per cup and a standard muffin pan about 8 tablespoons of batter per cup. Obviously, the smaller the muffin, the quicker it cooks, so you will have to adjust baking time. Most mini muffins take 10–12 minutes and standard ones 18–20 minutes.

Q – *My muffins are always slightly flat, even though I measure carefully and use fresh raising agents. Could my oven be at fault?*

A – Temperature is one of the secrets to well-risen, domed muffins. Make sure that the oven is completely heated before you bake your muffins and close the oven door as quickly as possible to keep the heat trapped. Try setting the oven temperature slightly higher initially, then lower it as soon as you've added the muffins. This extra heat will create a burst of steam to help raise the batter.

CHOCOLATE MUFFINS

VANILLA CHOCOLATE CHIP Muffins

If you prefer, make mini muffins (this recipe makes 36 mini muffins). Freeze them to pop into lunchboxes, or keep them in an airtight container for quick pop-in-the-mouth snacks.

MAKES 12

300g self-raising flour
1 teaspoon baking powder
50g butter
80g caster sugar
150g milk or plain chocolate chips
2 eggs, lightly beaten
225ml milk
1 teaspoon vanilla extract

MUFFIN TIP
For chunkier chocolate chip muffins, measure 150g from a bar/block of milk or plain chocolate, then cut it into small chunks using a sharp knife and use the chopped chocolate instead of the chocolate chips.

1. Preheat the oven to 200°C/400°F/Gas mark 6. Grease a 12-cup muffin tin or line the cups with paper muffin cases.

2. Mix the flour and baking powder in a large bowl. Rub in the butter until the mixture resembles fine breadcrumbs. Stir in the sugar and chocolate chips.

3. In a separate bowl or jug, mix together the eggs, milk and vanilla extract, then pour the milk mixture all at once into the dry ingredients. Mix briefly until just combined.

4. Spoon the batter into the prepared muffin cups, dividing it evenly. Bake in the oven for 18–20 minutes, or until well risen, golden and firm to the touch. Cool in the tin for 10 minutes, then turn out onto a wire rack. Serve warm or cold.

MARSHMALLOW, CHOC & COLA Muffins

Great for teenage parties and sleepovers, these chocolate muffins contain mini marshmallows. The cola not only flavours and sweetens the muffins, but the carbonation helps to lighten the batter.

MAKES 12

250g self-raising flour
2 tablespoons unsweetened cocoa powder
1 teaspoon baking powder
Pinch of salt
125g caster sugar
1 egg, lightly beaten
6 tablespoons vegetable oil
150ml cola
75g mini marshmallows

MUFFIN TIP
If mini marshmallows are not available, snip larger marshmallows into quarters using kitchen scissors dipped in icing sugar.

1. Preheat the oven to 190°C/375°F/Gas mark 5. Grease a 12-cup muffin tin or line the cups with paper muffin cases.

2. Mix the flour, cocoa powder, baking powder, salt and sugar in a large bowl. In a separate bowl or large jug, mix together the egg and vegetable oil. Add the cola (it will froth up, so make sure the container is large enough), then pour the cola mixture all at once into the dry ingredients and mix briefly until just combined.

3. Place a large spoonful of batter into each prepared muffin cup, then add three or four mini marshmallows, keeping them in the middle of the muffin. Spoon the remaining batter on top, dividing it evenly.

4. Bake in the oven for about 20 minutes, or until well risen and firm to the touch. Cool in the tin for 10 minutes, then turn out onto a wire rack. Serve warm or cold.

CHOCOLATE & BRANDY DESSERT Muffins

These dark chocolate muffins are served with a sweet and creamy white chocolate sauce.

MAKES 12

300g self-raising flour
1 teaspoon baking powder
50g unsweetened cocoa powder
225g caster sugar
1 egg, lightly beaten
175ml buttermilk
125g butter, melted
2 tablespoons brandy
Finely grated zest of 1 small orange
Fresh fruit, to serve
2 teaspoons icing sugar, sifted, to
   decorate

FOR THE WHITE CHOCOLATE SAUCE
200g white chocolate, broken into
   squares
6 tablespoons double cream
4 tablespoons single cream

1. Preheat the oven to 190°C/375°F/Gas mark 5. Grease a 12-cup non-stick muffin tin.

2. For the muffins, mix the flour, baking powder, cocoa powder and caster sugar in a large bowl. In a separate bowl or jug, mix together the egg, buttermilk, melted butter, brandy and orange zest. Add the wet ingredients to the dry ingredients and mix briefly until just combined.

3. Spoon the batter into the prepared muffin cups, dividing evenly. Bake in the oven for 18–20 minutes, or until well risen and firm to the touch. Cool in the tin for 5 minutes, then turn onto a wire rack to cool completely.

4. For the white chocolate sauce, melt the chocolate and 2 tablespoons of the double cream in a heat-proof bowl placed over a pan of hot, but not boiling water. Stir until smooth. Add the remaining double cream and the single cream and stir until blended. Remove from the heat and whisk the chocolate sauce until smooth.

5. Place a chocolate muffin on a plate and top with fresh fruit. Pour over a little of the warm white chocolate sauce, letting it dribble down the sides. Repeat with the remaining muffins. Dust with sifted icing sugar before serving.

RICH CHOCOLATE TRUFFLE MINI Muffins

MAKES 24

125g self-raising flour
3 tablespoons unsweetened cocoa
    powder
3/4 teaspoon baking powder
25g butter
50g caster sugar
1 egg, lightly beaten
100ml milk
1 tablespoon double cream
1 teaspoon vanilla extract
1 teaspoon icing sugar, to decorate

FOR THE CHOCOLATE GANACHE

75g plain or milk chocolate chips
5 tablespoons double cream

MUFFIN TIP
*To shorten the time the
ganache takes to thicken, chill
it in the fridge, stirring the
mixture occasionally.*

1. Preheat the oven to 200°C/400°F/Gas mark 6. Grease two 12-cup mini muffin tins or one 24-cup mini muffin tin, or line the cups with paper mini muffin cases.

2. For the muffins, mix the flour, cocoa powder and baking powder in a large bowl. Rub in the butter until the mixture resembles fine breadcrumbs. Stir in the caster sugar.

3. In a separate small bowl or jug, mix together the egg, milk, cream and vanilla extract, then pour the egg mixture all at once into the dry ingredients and mix briefly until just combined.

4. Spoon the batter into the prepared muffin cups, dividing evenly. Bake in the oven for 8–10 minutes, or until well risen and firm to the touch. Cool in the tins for 5 minutes, then turn onto a wire rack to cool completely.

5. While the muffins are baking, make the chocolate ganache. Put the chocolate chips in a small bowl. Bring the cream to the boil in a small saucepan. Pour the hot cream over the chocolate chips and stir until melted and smooth. Leave for about 1 hour to cool and thicken.

6. When the ganache is the consistency of softened butter, beat it for a few seconds, then spread a swirl of ganache on top of each muffin. Lightly dust the muffins with sifted icing sugar before serving.

WHITE CHOCOLATE & MACADAMIA NUT Muffins

These delicious moist chocolate muffins are studded with white chocolate and the king of nuts – macadamia nuts.

MAKES 12

175g plain chocolate, coarsely chopped or broken into squares
225g plain flour
150g soft light brown sugar
2 tablespoons unsweetened cocoa powder
1 teaspoon baking powder
1/2 teaspoon salt
175ml buttermilk
2 eggs, lightly beaten
1 1/2 teaspoons vanilla extract
200g white chocolate, chopped
100g unsalted macadamia nuts, coarsely chopped

MUFFIN TIP
Use chopped pistachios, hazelnuts or pecans instead of macadamia nuts, if you prefer. Use white chocolate chips instead of chopped white chocolate, if you like.

1. Preheat the oven to 200°C/400°F/Gas mark 6. Grease a 12-cup muffin tin or line the cups with paper muffin cases.

2. Melt the plain chocolate in a small heat-proof bowl placed over a pan of barely simmering water, stirring occasionally until melted and smooth; do not allow the bottom of the bowl to touch the water. Remove from the heat and set aside.

3. Mix the flour, sugar, cocoa powder, baking powder and salt in a large bowl. In a separate bowl or jug, mix together the buttermilk, eggs and vanilla extract.

4. Add the buttermilk mixture and the melted chocolate mixture to the dry ingredients and mix briefly until just combined. Fold in the white chocolate and macadamia nuts.

5. Spoon the batter into the prepared muffin cups, dividing it evenly. Bake in the oven for about 20 minutes, or until well risen and firm to the touch. Cool in the tin for 5 minutes, then turn out onto a wire rack. Serve warm or cold.

CHOCOLATE CHIP CRUMBLE Muffins

MUFFIN TIP
For chunkier chocolate muffins, use coarsely chopped plain or milk chocolate instead of chocolate chips.

These have a double dose of chocolate; the muffin mixture is packed with chocolate chips then generously topped with a chocolate crumble.

MAKES 12

250g self-raising flour
1 teaspoon baking powder
Pinch of salt
50g butter
100g soft light brown sugar
150g plain or milk chocolate chips
2 eggs, lightly beaten
225ml milk
2 teaspoons vanilla extract

FOR THE CHOCOLATE CRUMBLE TOPPING
50g plain flour
1 tablespoon unsweetened
  cocoa powder
40g butter
2 tablespoons caster sugar

1. Preheat the oven to 200°C/400°F/Gas mark 6. Grease a 12-cup muffin tin or line the cups with paper muffin cases.

2. For the chocolate crumble topping, sift the flour and cocoa powder into a bowl. Rub in the butter until the mixture resembles coarse breadcrumbs, then stir in the sugar. Set aside.

3. For the muffins, mix the flour, baking powder and salt in a large bowl. Rub in the butter until the mixture resembles fine breadcrumbs. Stir in the sugar and chocolate chips.

4. In a separate bowl or jug, mix together the eggs, milk and vanilla extract. Pour the milk mixture all at once into the dry ingredients and mix briefly until just combined.

5. Spoon the batter into the prepared muffin cups, dividing it evenly, then sprinkle the tops with the crumble topping. Bake in the oven for 18–20 minutes, or until well risen and firm to the touch. Cool in the tin for 5 minutes, then turn out onto a wire rack. Serve warm or cold.

DARK CHOCOLATE & GINGER Muffins

MAKES 10

200g plain chocolate, roughly
   chopped
75g butter
300g self-raising flour
150g soft light brown sugar
$3/4$ teaspoon bicarbonate of soda
Pinch of salt
50g preserved stem ginger, drained
   and finely chopped
175ml soured cream
3 tablespoons golden syrup
1 egg, lightly beaten
2 teaspoons vanilla extract
50g white chocolate, broken
   into squares
Extra chopped preserved stem ginger,
   to decorate

MUFFIN TIP
*For a simple finish, dust
these muffins with a little
sifted icing sugar and
unsweetened cocoa powder,
if you prefer.*

1. Preheat the oven to 200°C/400°F/Gas mark 6. Grease 10 cups of a 12-cup muffin tin or line 10 cups with paper muffin cases.

2. Melt the plain chocolate and butter together in a medium heat-proof bowl placed over a pan of barely simmering water, stirring occasionally until smooth. Remove from the heat and cool for a few minutes.

3. Mix the flour, sugar, bicarbonate of soda, salt and stem ginger in a large bowl. In a separate bowl or jug, mix together the soured cream, golden syrup, egg and vanilla extract, then add the melted chocolate mixture and stir until blended. Add the wet ingredients to the dry ingredients and mix briefly until just combined.

4. Spoon the batter into the prepared muffin cups, dividing evenly. Bake in the oven for about 20 minutes, or until risen and firm to the touch. Cool in the tin for 10 minutes, then turn onto a wire rack to cool completely.

5. Melt the white chocolate in a small heat-proof bowl placed over a pan of barely simmering water, stirring occasionally until smooth. Spoon the melted white chocolate into a small greaseproof paper piping bag, snip off the end and pipe zig-zags of chocolate over the tops of the muffins. Scatter a few pieces of chopped stem ginger over each and leave to set before serving.

WHITE CHOCOLATE, LEMON & RASPBERRY Muffins

Small chunks of white chocolate, grated lemon zest and fresh raspberries combine to create these really tasty muffins, ideal for a mid-morning or afternoon snack.

MAKES 12

300g self-raising flour
1 teaspoon baking powder
50g butter
80g caster sugar
100g fresh raspberries
150g white chocolate, coarsely
  chopped
Finely grated zest of 1 lemon
2 eggs, lightly beaten
225ml milk

1. Preheat the oven to 200°C/400°F/Gas mark 6. Grease a 12-cup muffin tin or line the cups with paper muffin cases.

2. Mix the flour and baking powder in a large bowl. Rub in the butter until the mixture resembles fine breadcrumbs. Stir in the sugar, raspberries, white chocolate and lemon zest.

3. In a separate bowl or jug, mix together the eggs and milk, then pour the egg mixture all at once into the dry ingredients and mix briefly until just combined.

4. Spoon the batter into the prepared muffin cups, dividing it evenly. Bake in the oven for 18–20 minutes, or until well risen, golden and firm to the touch. Cool in the tin for 5 minutes, then turn out onto a wire rack. Serve warm or cold.

MUFFIN TIP
You can use frozen raspberries in this recipe if fresh are not available. You don't even need to thaw them first.

DOUBLE CHOCOLATE CHIP Muffins

These delicious muffins are for true chocolate lovers who just can't get enough chocolate. Serve them freshly baked and warm from the oven for a real chocolatey treat.

MAKES 12

300g plain flour
200g soft light brown sugar
2 tablespoons unsweetened cocoa powder
2 teaspoons bicarbonate of soda
$1/2$ teaspoon salt
350ml milk
75g butter or margarine, melted
2 eggs, lightly beaten
150g plain chocolate chips

1. Preheat the oven to 200°C/400°F/Gas mark 6. Grease a 12-cup muffin tin or line the cups with paper muffin cases.

2. Mix the flour, sugar, cocoa powder, bicarbonate of soda and salt in a large bowl. In a separate bowl or jug, mix together the milk, melted butter or margarine and eggs.

3. Add the wet ingredients all at once to the dry ingredients and mix briefly until just combined. Fold in the chocolate chips.

4. Spoon the batter into the prepared muffin cups, dividing it evenly. Bake in the oven for about 20 minutes, or until well risen. Cool in the tin for 5 minutes, then turn out onto a wire rack. Serve warm or cold.

MINTED CHOCOLATE
Muffins

Ideal for St. Patrick's Day, these chocolate muffins have chocolate mints folded into the mixture and are topped with minty cream icing and pistachio nuts.

MAKES 10

250g plain flour
2 tablespoons unsweetened cocoa
   powder
2 teaspoons baking powder
$\frac{1}{2}$ teaspoon bicarbonate of soda
100g soft light brown sugar
150g chocolate mints or mint-
   flavoured chocolate, roughly
   chopped
1 egg, separated
Pinch of salt
85g butter, melted
125ml soured cream
125ml milk

FOR THE MINT CREAM ICING

125ml whipping cream
$\frac{1}{4}$ teaspoon peppermint essence
1–2 drops green food colouring
4 tablespoons caster sugar
100g pistachio nuts, chopped

1. Preheat the oven to 200°C/400°F/Gas mark 6. Grease 10 cups of a 12-cup muffin tin or line 10 cups with paper muffin cases.

2. For the muffins, mix the flour, cocoa powder, baking powder, bicarbonate of soda, sugar and chocolate mints or mint-flavoured chocolate in a large bowl.

3. Put the egg white and salt in a clean bowl and whisk until soft peaks form. In a separate bowl or jug, mix together the egg yolk, melted butter, soured cream and milk. Pour the milk mixture all at once into the dry ingredients and mix briefly until almost combined. Add the whisked egg white and gently fold into the mixture until combined.

4. Spoon the batter into the prepared muffin cups, dividing evenly. Bake in the oven for 18–20 minutes, or until well risen and firm to the touch. Cool in the tin for 10 minutes, then turn onto a wire rack to cool completely.

5. To make the icing, whip the cream in a bowl until soft peaks form. Add the peppermint essence and a drop or two of green food colouring, then whisk in the sugar a spoonful at a time until the mixture is fairly stiff. Spoon or pipe the minted-cream icing on top of the muffins, then scatter over the pistachio nuts. Serve within 1 hour of icing.

CHOCOLATE MALT
Muffins

Malted milk powder adds a subtle flavour to these chocolate muffins.
They make a delicious bed-time treat, served while still warm.

MAKES 10

250g self-raising flour
3 tablespoons unsweetened
   cocoa powder
2 tablespoons malted milk
   powder e.g. Horlicks
1 teaspoon baking powder
1/4 teaspoon bicarbonate of soda
1/2 teaspoon salt
110g caster sugar
1 egg, lightly beaten
225ml milk
2 teaspoons vanilla extract
75g butter, melted

1. Preheat the oven to 190°C/375°F/Gas mark 5. Grease 10 cups of a
12-cup muffin tin or line 10 cups with paper muffin cases.

2. Mix the flour, cocoa powder, malted milk powder, baking powder,
bicarbonate of soda, salt and sugar in a large bowl. In a separate bowl or
jug, mix together the egg, milk, vanilla extract and melted butter.

3. Add the wet ingredients all at once to the dry ingredients and mix
briefly until just combined.

4. Spoon the batter into the prepared muffin cups, dividing it evenly.
Bake in the oven for about 20 minutes, or until well risen and firm to the
touch. Cool in the tin for 5 minutes, then turn out
onto a wire rack. Serve warm or cold.

MUFFIN TIP
*If you prefer, use
6 tablespoons of
sunflower oil instead of
the melted butter.*

BANANA, WALNUT & CHOC-CHIP Muffins

These muffins are really lovely served warm, when the chocolate and banana have that soft, melt-in-the-mouth quality.

MAKES 12

300g self-raising flour
2 tablespoons soft light brown sugar
60g walnuts, chopped
100g plain chocolate chips
2 ripe bananas (250g total weight), peeled
3 tablespoons vegetable oil
2 eggs, lightly beaten
125ml soured cream

1. Preheat the oven to 200°C/400°F/Gas mark 6. Grease a 12-cup muffin tin or line the cups with paper muffin cases.

2. Mix together the flour, sugar, walnuts and chocolate chips in a large bowl. In a separate bowl, mash the bananas until fairly smooth, then stir in the vegetable oil, eggs and soured cream.

3. Add the wet ingredients all at once to the dry ingredients, and mix briefly until just combined.

4. Spoon the batter into the prepared muffin cups, dividing it evenly. Bake in the oven for about 20 minutes, or until risen and golden. Cool in the tin for 10 minutes, then turn out onto a wire rack. Serve warm or cold.

BLACK FOREST Muffins

MAKES 10

150g butter
150g caster sugar
4 eggs, separated
1 teaspoon vanilla extract
125g plain flour
25g unsweetened cocoa powder
1 teaspoon baking powder
75g morello cherries in syrup (in a
   jar), well-drained

FOR THE CHERRY SYRUP &
DECORATION
2 tablespoons caster sugar
2 tablespoons syrup from a jar of
   morello cherries
2 tablespoons kirsch or cherry liqueur
150ml double or whipping cream
1 tablespoon icing sugar
10 morello cherries
Chocolate curls, to decorate

1. Preheat the oven to 180°C/350°F/Gas mark 4. Grease 10 cups of a 12-cup muffin tin or line 10 cups with paper muffin cases.

2. For the muffins, melt the butter and sugar in a heavy-based saucepan over a very low heat. Bring the mixture to a gentle boil and cook for 2 minutes, stirring constantly. Remove the pan from the heat and leave to cool, then transfer the mixture to a large mixing bowl. Set aside.

3. Put the egg whites in a clean bowl and whisk until soft peaks form, then set aside. Stir the egg yolks and vanilla extract into the cooled butter and sugar, then sift over the flour, cocoa powder and baking powder and gently fold in with the morello cherries. Fold in the whisked egg whites.

4. Spoon the batter into the prepared muffin cups, dividing it evenly. Bake in the oven for 15–18 minutes, or until well risen and firm to the touch. Cool in the tin for 5 minutes, then transfer to a wire rack.

5. Meanwhile, make the syrup. Gently heat the caster sugar and morello cherry syrup in a small saucepan, stirring until the sugar has dissolved. Remove the pan from the heat and stir in 1 tablespoon of the kirsch or cherry liqueur. Drizzle a little syrup over the top of each warm muffin.

6. Whip the cream in a bowl with the remaining kirsch or cherry liqueur and the icing sugar until soft peaks form, then spoon the mixture into a piping bag fitted with a large star nozzle. Pipe a swirl of flavoured cream on top of each cooled muffin and decorate with a morello cherry and a few chocolate curls. Chill until ready to serve.

CHOCOLATE-FILLED
Muffins

These hazelnut-topped muffins hide a delicious rich chocolate centre to create a tempting sweet treat.

MAKES 12

300g self-raising flour
1 teaspoon baking powder
50g butter
80g caster sugar
2 eggs, lightly beaten
225ml milk
1 teaspoon vanilla extract
2 tablespoons finely chopped
 hazelnuts
1 tablespoon demerara sugar

FOR THE FILLING

20g butter, softened
75g icing sugar
1¹/₂ teaspoons milk
¹/₂ teaspoon vanilla extract
50g plain chocolate, melted

1. Preheat the oven to 200°C/400°F/Gas mark 6. Grease a 12-cup muffin tin or line the cups with paper muffin cases.

2. For the filling, cream the butter in a small bowl. Gradually add the icing sugar, beating until well mixed. Beat in the milk, vanilla extract and melted chocolate until well combined. Set aside.

3. For the muffins, mix the flour and baking powder in a large bowl. Rub in the butter until the mixture resembles fine breadcrumbs. Stir in the caster sugar. In a separate bowl or jug, mix together the eggs, milk and vanilla extract. Pour the egg mixture all at once into the dry ingredients and mix briefly until just combined.

4. Put a spoonful of the batter into each prepared muffin cup. Drop a large teaspoonful of the filling mixture on top of each, then cover with the remaining muffin batter, dividing it evenly.

5. Mix together the chopped hazelnuts and demerara sugar and sprinkle this mixture evenly over the tops of the muffins.

6. Bake in the oven for 18–20 minutes, or until well risen, golden and firm to the touch. Cool in the tin for 5 minutes, then turn out onto a wire rack. These muffins are best served warm.

CAPPUCCINO Muffins

Don't be tempted to substitute instant coffee for ground coffee in this recipe. If possible, use a rich, dark roasted variety of coffee for the best flavour.

MAKES 12

115g self-raising flour
185g plain flour
1 tablespoon baking powder
1/2 teaspoon salt
60g unsweetened cocoa powder
100g soft light brown sugar
2 tablespoons finely ground coffee
75g butter, softened
225ml soured cream
225ml whipping cream
2 eggs, lightly beaten
Finely grated zest of 2 oranges
125g dark bitter chocolate, coarsely
    chopped

1. Preheat the oven to 180°C/350°F/Gas mark 4. Grease a 12-cup muffin tin or line the cups with paper muffin cases.

2. Mix the flours, baking powder, salt and cocoa powder in a large bowl. Stir in the sugar and ground coffee.

3. In a separate bowl or jug, beat together the butter, soured cream, whipping cream and eggs. Add the wet ingredients to the dry ingredients along with the orange zest and chocolate and mix until just combined.

4. Spoon the batter into the prepared muffin cups, dividing it evenly. Bake in the oven for 15–20 minutes, or until risen and firm to the touch. Cool in the tin for 10 minutes, then turn out onto a wire rack. Serve warm or cold.

SPECKLED CHOCOLATE Muffins

These muffins contain oats soaked in vanilla-flavoured milk, which gives them a lovely texture. The speckled appearance is achieved by stirring coarsely grated or finely chopped chocolate into the mixture.

MAKES 10

50g rolled oats
275ml milk
2 teaspoons vanilla extract
250g plain flour
1 tablespoon baking powder
½ teaspoon salt
110g caster sugar
150g plain chocolate, coarsely grated or very finely chopped
1 egg, lightly beaten
100g butter, melted

1. Preheat the oven to 200°C/400°F/Gas mark 6. Grease 10 cups of a 12-cup muffin tin or line 10 cups with paper muffin cases.

2. Put the oats in a bowl and pour over the milk and vanilla extract. Stir, then leave to soak while you prepare the remaining ingredients.

3. Mix the flour, baking powder, salt and sugar in a large bowl. Stir in the chocolate. Stir the egg and melted butter into the soaked oat mixture. Add the oat mixture all at once to the dry ingredients and mix briefly until just combined.

4. Spoon the batter into the prepared muffin cups, dividing it evenly. Bake in the oven for 18–20 minutes, or until risen and golden. Cool in the tin for 10 minutes, then turn out onto a wire rack. Serve warm or cold.

MUFFIN TIP
A mixture of plain, milk and white chocolate can be used to give the muffins a marbled effect.

GLAZED MOCHA CHOC-CHIP Muffins

MAKES 12

300g self-raising flour
1 teaspoon baking powder
50g butter
80g caster sugar
150g plain chocolate chips or plain
  chocolate, chopped
2 eggs, lightly beaten
150ml milk
5 tablespoons fresh espresso
  coffee, cooled

FOR THE CHOCOLATE GLAZE
25g butter
2 tablespoons unsweetened
  cocoa powder
2 tablespoons fresh espresso, cooled
150g icing sugar, sifted
1/2 teaspoon vanilla extract

1. Preheat the oven to 200°C/400°F/Gas mark 6. Grease a 12-cup muffin tin or line the cups with paper muffin cases.

2. For the muffins, mix the flour and baking powder in a large bowl. Rub in the butter until the mixture resembles fine breadcrumbs. Stir in the sugar and chocolate chips or chopped chocolate. In a separate bowl or jug, mix together the eggs, milk and espresso. Pour this mixture all at once into the dry ingredients and mix briefly until just combined.

3. Spoon the batter into the prepared muffin cups, dividing it evenly. Bake in the oven for 18–20 minutes, or until well risen and firm to the touch. Cool in the tin for 5 minutes, then turn out onto a wire rack and leave to cool completely.

4. For the chocolate glaze, melt the butter in a small saucepan over a low heat. Add the cocoa powder and espresso coffee, stirring constantly until the mixture thickens; do not boil. Remove the pan from the heat and slowly add the icing sugar and vanilla extract, beating until smooth. If necessary, thin the glaze with a little hot water until it is thin enough to drizzle over the cooled muffins. Leave the glazed muffins to stand for about 30 minutes, or until set, before serving.

TRIPLE CHOCOLATE CHUNK Muffins

These chocolate-packed muffins are given a lighter touch by folding whisked egg white into the mixture before baking.

MAKES 10

250g plain flour
2 teaspoons baking powder
½ teaspoon bicarbonate of soda
100g soft light brown sugar
50g plain chocolate, roughly chopped
50g milk chocolate, roughly chopped
50g white chocolate, roughly chopped
1 egg, separated
¼ teaspoon salt
85g butter, melted
50ml soured cream
175ml milk
1 teaspoon vanilla extract

1. Preheat the oven to 200°C/400°F/Gas mark 6. Grease 10 cups of a 12-cup muffin tin or line 10 cups with paper muffin cases.

2. Mix the flour, baking powder, bicarbonate of soda, sugar and about two-thirds of each type of chocolate in a large bowl.

3. Put the egg white and salt in a clean bowl and whisk until soft peaks form. In a separate bowl or jug, mix together the egg yolk, melted butter, soured cream, milk and vanilla extract. Pour the milk mixture all at once into the dry ingredients and mix briefly until almost combined. Add the whisked egg white and gently fold into the mixture until combined.

4. Spoon the batter into the prepared muffin cups, dividing it evenly, then gently press the remaining mixed chocolate on top of the muffins. Bake in the oven for 18–20 minutes, or until well risen and firm to the touch. Cool in the tin for 10 minutes, then turn out onto a wire rack. Serve warm or cold.

MUFFIN TIP
If you prefer, use just one or two types of chocolate. Flavoured chocolates, such as orange, mint or hazelnut varieties, would also work well.

CHOCOLATE RUM & RAISIN Muffins

If time allows, soak the raisins in rum overnight so that they are really plump and well flavoured.

MAKES 10

150g raisins
2 tablespoons dark rum
250g plain flour
3 tablespoons unsweetened
    cocoa powder
1 tablespoon baking powder
Pinch of salt
Pinch of freshly grated nutmeg
150g caster sugar
150g plain chocolate, coarsely
    chopped
1 egg, lightly beaten
150ml milk
6 tablespoons vegetable oil

1. Put the raisins in a small bowl, pour over the rum and stir to coat. Cover and leave to soak for at least 15 minutes. Preheat the oven to 190°C/375°F/Gas mark 5. Grease 10 cups of a 12-cup muffin tin or line 10 cups with paper muffin cases.

2. Mix the flour, cocoa powder, baking powder, salt, nutmeg, sugar and chocolate in a large bowl. In a separate bowl or jug, mix together the egg, milk, vegetable oil and rum-soaked raisins. Add the raisin mixture all at once to the dry ingredients and mix briefly until just combined.

3. Spoon the batter into the prepared muffin cups, dividing it evenly. Bake in the oven for about 20 minutes, or until risen and firm to the touch. Cool in the tin for 10 minutes, then turn out onto a wire rack. Serve warm or cold.

MUFFIN TIP
If you prefer, use an orange-flavoured liqueur instead of the rum, or simply soak the raisins in fruit juice.

CHOCOLATE ALMOND Muffins

These rich chocolate muffins are studded with small pieces of marzipan, keeping their texture soft and moist. A scattering of flaked almonds gives them a lavish finish.

MAKES 12

225g self-raising flour
3 tablespoons unsweetened cocoa powder
1 teaspoon baking powder
Pinch of salt
50g butter
125g caster sugar
100g marzipan, cut into small cubes
2 eggs, lightly beaten
225ml milk
¼ teaspoon almond extract
25g flaked almonds

MUFFIN TIP
Instead of flaked almonds, scatter 100g coarsely grated marzipan over the tops of the muffins before baking. Cover the muffins with foil after 12 minutes baking time to prevent the marzipan from over-browning.

1. Preheat the oven to 190°C/375°F/Gas mark 5. Grease a 12-cup muffin tin or line the cups with paper muffin cases.

2. Mix the flour, cocoa powder, baking powder and salt in a large bowl. Rub in the butter until the mixture resembles fine breadcrumbs. Stir in the sugar and marzipan.

3. In a separate bowl or jug, mix together the eggs, milk and almond extract. Pour the milk mixture all at once into the dry ingredients and mix briefly until just combined.

4. Spoon the batter into the prepared muffin cups, dividing it evenly, then sprinkle the tops with flaked almonds. Bake in the oven for about 20 minutes, or until well risen and firm to the touch. Cool in the tin for 10 minutes, then turn out onto a wire rack. Serve warm or cold.

CHOCOLATE FUDGE
Muffins

These delicious muffins pack a real chocolate punch and are definitely not for the faint-hearted.

MAKES 12

150g plain chocolate, coarsely chopped
50g dark bitter chocolate, coarsely chopped
75g butter
300g plain flour
150g soft light brown sugar
1 teaspoon bicarbonate of soda
1/4 teaspoon salt
175ml soured cream
3 tablespoons golden syrup
1 egg, lightly beaten
1 1/4 teaspoons vanilla extract
100g plain chocolate chips

1. Preheat the oven to 200°C/400°F/Gas mark 6. Grease a 12-cup muffin tin or line the cups with paper muffin cases.

2. Melt the plain chocolate, bitter chocolate and butter together in a heat-proof bowl placed over a pan of barely simmering water, stirring occasionally until smooth. Remove from the heat and cool slightly.

3. Mix the flour, sugar, bicarbonate of soda and salt in a large bowl. In a separate small bowl or jug, mix together the soured cream, golden syrup, egg and vanilla extract, then fold this into the melted chocolate mixture. Fold in the chocolate chips. Add the chocolate mixture to the dry ingredients, mixing briefly until just combined.

4. Spoon the batter into the prepared muffin cups, dividing it evenly. Bake in the oven for about 20 minutes, or until well risen and firm to the touch. Cool in the tin for 5 minutes, then turn out onto a wire rack. Serve warm or cold.

MUFFIN TIP
Dark bitter chocolate with a cocoa solids content of 70% (minimum) would work well in this recipe.

CHOCOLATE CHIP & ORANGE Muffins

The orange zest adds a lovely freshness to these muffins, for those who may otherwise find chocolate muffins a little too rich.

MAKES 12

300g plain flour
200g soft light brown sugar
2 tablespoons unsweetened cocoa powder
2 teaspoons bicarbonate of soda
½ teaspoon salt
100g plain chocolate chips
225ml milk
75g butter or margarine, melted
2 eggs, lightly beaten
Finely grated zest of 1 orange

1. Preheat the oven to 200°C/400°F/Gas mark 6. Grease a 12-cup muffin tin or line the cups with paper muffin cases.

2. Mix the flour, sugar, cocoa powder, bicarbonate of soda, salt and chocolate chips in a large bowl.

3. In a separate bowl or jug, mix together the milk, melted butter or margarine, eggs and orange zest. Add the wet ingredients to the dry ingredients and mix briefly until just combined.

4. Spoon the batter into the prepared muffin cups, dividing it evenly. Bake in the oven for about 20 minutes, or until well risen and firm to the touch. Cool in the tin for 5 minutes, then turn out onto a wire rack. Serve warm or cold.

CHOCOLATE CHEESECAKE Muffins

A lovely cheesecake topping mixture is swirled into the muffin batter to create these delicious almond-topped chocolate muffins.

MAKES 12

150g plain flour
175g caster sugar
35g unsweetened cocoa powder
1/2 teaspoon bicarbonate of soda
1/4 teaspoon salt
125ml soured cream
3 tablespoons vegetable oil
50g butter, melted and cooled
2 eggs, lightly beaten
1 teaspoon vanilla extract
75g plain chocolate, melted
25g flaked almonds

FOR THE CHEESECAKE MIXTURE

175g cream cheese or full-fat soft
   cheese, at room temperature
60g caster sugar
1 egg, lightly beaten
1/8 teaspoon vanilla extract

1. Preheat the oven to 190°C/375°F/Gas mark 5. Grease a 12-cup muffin tin or line the cups with paper muffin cases.

2. For the cheesecake mixture, combine the cream cheese or soft cheese, sugar, egg and vanilla extract in a bowl. Set aside.

3. For the muffins, mix the flour, sugar, cocoa powder, bicarbonate of soda and salt in a large bowl. In a separate bowl or jug, mix together the soured cream, vegetable oil, melted butter, eggs, vanilla extract and melted chocolate. Add the wet ingredients to the dry ingredients and mix briefly until just combined.

4. Spoon the batter into the prepared muffin cups, dividing it evenly, then carefully spoon a little of the cheesecake mixture over the chocolate batter in each muffin cup. Swirl the mixture slightly with a knife so the batter appears marbled. Sprinkle the tops with flaked almonds.

5. Bake in the oven for 20–25 minutes, or until risen and firm to the touch. Cool in the tin for 5 minutes, then turn out onto a wire rack. Serve warm or cold.

FRUIT
MUFFINS

PEAR & WALNUT Muffins with Butterscotch Sauce

These lightly spiced fruit and nut muffins, drizzled with butterscotch sauce, create a lovely dessert or sweet treat.

MAKES 12

300g plain flour
2 teaspoons baking powder
$^1/_2$ teaspoon bicarbonate of soda
225g caster sugar
$^1/_4$ teaspoon salt
1 teaspoon ground cinnamon
1 teaspoon ground cardamom
2 eggs, lightly beaten
175ml soured cream
175g butter, melted
3 canned pear halves in fruit juice,
    drained and diced
65g walnuts, coarsely chopped
FOR THE BUTTERSCOTCH SAUCE
200g soft dark brown sugar
125g butter
4 tablespoons whipping cream

1. Preheat the oven to 200°C/400°F/Gas mark 6. Grease a 12-cup muffin tin or line the cups with paper muffin cases.

2. For the muffins, mix the flour, baking powder, bicarbonate of soda, sugar, salt, cinnamon and cardamom in a large bowl.

3. In a separate bowl or jug, whisk together the eggs, soured cream and melted butter. Add the wet ingredients to the dry ingredients along with the pears and walnuts and mix briefly until just combined.

4. Spoon the batter into the prepared muffin cups, dividing it evenly. Bake in the oven for about 20 minutes, or until risen and golden.

5. Meanwhile, for the butterscotch sauce, combine the sugar and butter in a saucepan and place over a low heat until the butter has melted and sugar has dissolved, stirring occasionally; do not allow the mixture to boil. Remove the pan from the heat and add the cream. Mix well and keep warm.

6. When the muffins are baked, cool them in the tin for 10 minutes, then turn onto a wire rack. Serve warm drizzled with the butterscotch sauce.

MARMALADE MORNING Muffins

Perfect for breakfast, these marmalade-flavoured muffins are made with wholemeal flour, sunflower margarine and juicy chunks of fresh pear, making them a healthy start to the day.

MAKES 12

75g plain wholemeal flour
225g plain white flour
175g golden caster sugar
1 tablespoon baking powder
½ teaspoon salt
2 eggs, lightly beaten
2 tablespoons orange marmalade
175ml unsweetened orange juice
125g sunflower margarine, melted
2 medium ripe pears, peeled, cored and chopped

FOR THE TOPPING
1 tablespoon unsweetened orange juice
4 tablespoons orange marmalade

1. Preheat the oven to 200°C/400°F/Gas mark 6. Grease a 12-cup muffin tin or line the cups with paper muffin cases.

2. For the muffins, mix the flours, sugar, baking powder and salt in a large bowl. In a separate bowl or jug, mix together the eggs, marmalade, orange juice, melted margarine and two-thirds of the chopped pears. Add the wet ingredients to the dry ingredients, mixing briefly until just combined.

3. Spoon the batter into the prepared muffin cups, dividing it evenly. Scatter with the remaining chopped pears, pressing the pieces gently into the batter. Bake in the oven for about 20 minutes, or until risen and golden. Cool in the tin for 5 minutes, then turn out onto a wire rack.

4. Meanwhile, for the topping, gently heat the orange juice and marmalade together in a small saucepan, stirring occasionally until melted and combined. Spoon and brush over the tops of the warm muffins. Serve warm.

OVERNIGHT Muffins

This fruity muffin mixture improves if left for at least 8 hours or overnight in the fridge. It's therefore ideal for making brunch-time muffins or for days when you know you'll be really busy.

MAKES 12

225g plain flour
25g oat bran
100g unsweetened muesli
100g soft light brown sugar
1½ teaspoons ground cinnamon
1 teaspoon bicarbonate of soda
90g ready-to-eat dried apricots or
    dried dates, chopped
1 egg, lightly beaten
375ml buttermilk
125ml vegetable oil
2 tablespoons demerara sugar, to
    decorate

1. Mix the flour, oat bran, muesli, brown sugar, cinnamon, bicarbonate of soda and dried apricots or dates in a large bowl. In a separate bowl or jug, mix together the egg, buttermilk and vegetable oil.

2. Pour the wet ingredients into the dry ingredients and mix briefly until just combined. Cover the bowl with cling film and refrigerate for at least 8 hours, or overnight.

3. When ready to bake, preheat the oven to 190°C/375°F/Gas mark 5. Grease a 12-cup muffin tin or line the cups with paper muffin cases.

4. Spoon the batter into the prepared muffin cups, dividing it evenly. Sprinkle the demerara sugar evenly over the tops of the muffins. Bake in the oven for about 20 minutes, or until risen and firm. Cool in the tin for 10 minutes, then turn out onto a wire rack. Serve warm or cold.

MUFFIN TIP
Ring the changes by using your favourite dried fruit in the muffins; cranberries, blueberries and chopped tropical fruits would all work well.

MIXED BERRY Muffins

If fresh berries are not available, you can use frozen berries in this recipe; there's no need to thaw them first.

MAKES 12

300g self-raising flour
1 teaspoon baking powder
150g caster sugar
100g white chocolate, finely chopped
100g fresh raspberries
150g fresh blueberries
1 egg, lightly beaten
125g butter, melted
175ml buttermilk
3 tablespoons milk
1 teaspoon vanilla extract
2 teaspoons icing sugar, to decorate

1. Preheat the oven to 200°C/400°F/Gas mark 6. Grease a 12-cup muffin tin or line the cups with paper muffin cases.

2. Mix the flour, baking powder, caster sugar and chocolate in a large bowl. Scatter two-thirds of each of the raspberries and blueberries over the dry ingredients.

3. In a separate bowl or jug, mix together the egg, melted butter, buttermilk, milk and vanilla extract. Add the buttermilk mixture all at once to the dry ingredients and mix briefly until just combined.

4. Spoon the batter into the prepared muffin cups, dividing it evenly, then top with the remaining berries, pressing them gently into the batter. Bake in the oven for about 20 minutes, or until risen and golden. Cool in the tin for 10 minutes, then turn out onto a wire rack. Serve warm or cold, dusted with sifted icing sugar.

MUFFIN TIP
If buttermilk is unavailable, stir 1 teaspoon of lemon juice or white vinegar into 175ml semi-skimmed milk and leave to stand for about 1 hour before using.

MUESLI-TOPPED APPLE SAUCE Muffins

Using ready-made apple sauce and muesli means that these muffins are quick and easy to make, but you can of course prepare either, or both, yourself if you prefer.

MAKES 12

300g plain flour
100g soft light brown sugar
1 tablespoon baking powder
1/2 teaspoon bicarbonate of soda
1/2 teaspoon salt
1/2 teaspoon ground cinnamon
1/2 teaspoon freshly grated nutmeg
50g butter, melted
300g ready-made apple sauce
50ml milk
1 egg, lightly beaten
75g unsweetened muesli

1. Preheat the oven to 220°C/425°F/Gas mark 7. Grease a 12-cup muffin tin or line the cups with paper muffin cases.

2. Mix the flour, sugar, baking powder, bicarbonate of soda, salt, cinnamon and nutmeg in a large bowl. In a separate bowl or jug, mix together the melted butter, apple sauce, milk and egg. Add the wet ingredients to the dry ingredients and mix briefly until just combined. Spoon the batter into the prepared muffin cups, dividing it evenly.

3. Place the muesli in a bowl and crush lightly, using the back of a spoon or the end of a rolling pin, until the pieces are small and even. Sprinkle the crushed muesli evenly over the muffins.

4. Bake in the oven for 15–20 minutes, or until risen and golden. Cool in the tin for 10 minutes, then turn out onto a wire rack. Serve warm or cold.

MUFFIN TIP
*Use a muesli with raisins
or other dried fruit and nuts
for added crunch and
sweetness, but make sure
that it is unsweetened.*

RASPBERRY CHEESECAKE
Muffins

MAKES 12

FOR THE CHEESECAKE MIXTURE
150g cream cheese or full-fat soft
  cheese, softened
160g caster sugar
1 egg
½ teaspoon vanilla extract
FOR THE MUFFINS
225ml milk
75g butter
1 teaspoon vanilla extract
2 eggs, lightly beaten
225g plain flour
125g caster sugar
2 teaspoons baking powder
½ teaspoon salt
100g fresh or frozen raspberries

1. Preheat the oven to 200°C/400°F/Gas mark 6. Grease a 12-cup muffin tin or line the cups with paper muffin cases.

2. For the cheesecake mixture, combine the cream cheese or soft cheese, sugar, egg and vanilla extract in a bowl, mixing well. Set aside.

3. For the muffins, combine the milk, butter and vanilla extract in a saucepan and heat gently, stirring, until the butter is melted. Remove the pan from the heat and allow to cool. Beat in the eggs.

4. Mix the flour, sugar, baking powder and salt in a large bowl. Add the milk mixture to the dry ingredients and mix briefly until just combined. Gently fold in the raspberries.

5. Spoon the batter into the prepared muffin cups, dividing it evenly. Top each muffin with 2 teaspoons of the cream cheese mixture and swirl slightly with a knife. Bake in the oven for about 20 minutes, or until the tops spring back when lightly touched. Cool in the tin for 10 minutes, then turn out onto a wire rack. Serve warm or cold.

CRANBERRY & PECAN
Muffins

These cinnamon-spiced muffins would also be very tasty with juicy raisins or sultanas in place of the cranberries, if you prefer.

MAKES 12

300g plain flour
100g soft light brown sugar
50g granulated sugar
2 teaspoons baking powder
1 teaspoon salt
1 teaspoon ground cinnamon
275ml milk
125ml vegetable oil
1 egg, lightly beaten
150g dried cranberries
50g pecans, chopped

1. Preheat the oven to 180°C/350°F/Gas mark 4. Grease a 12-cup muffin tin or line the cups with paper muffin cases.

2. Combine the flour, sugars, baking powder, salt and cinnamon in a bowl. In a separate bowl or jug, mix together the milk, vegetable oil and egg.

3. Add the wet ingredients to the dry ingredients, mixing briefly until just combined. Gently fold in the cranberries and pecans.

4. Spoon the batter into the prepared muffin cups, dividing it evenly. Bake in the oven for about 25 minutes, or until risen and golden. Cool in the tin for 5 minutes, then turn out onto a wire rack. Serve warm or cold.

MUFFIN TIP
Use ground mixed spice or ground ginger in place of ground cinnamon for a tasty alternative.

APRICOT, VANILLA & LEMON Muffins

These are classy muffins, with a beautiful fresh vanilla fragrance. They are delicious served warm for a mid-morning snack or an afternoon treat.

MAKES 12

½ vanilla pod
225g caster sugar
300g plain flour
1 tablespoon baking powder
¾ teaspoon salt
125g butter, diced
100g ready-to-eat dried apricots, chopped
Finely grated zest of 1 lemon
1 egg, lightly beaten
225ml milk

MUFFIN TIP
If you don't have a vanilla pod, add 1 teaspoon of good quality vanilla extract to the wet ingredients and add the sugar to the dry ingredients.

1. Preheat the oven to 200°C/400°F/Gas mark 6. Grease a 12-cup muffin tin or line the cups with paper muffin cases.

2. Put the vanilla pod and sugar into a blender or food processor and blend until the vanilla pod is very finely chopped. Mix the flour, baking powder and salt in a large bowl, then stir in the vanilla sugar. Rub in the butter until the mixture resembles fine breadcrumbs. Stir in the dried apricots and lemon zest.

3. In a separate small bowl or jug, combine the egg and milk, then add this to the flour mixture, mixing briefly until just combined.

4. Spoon the batter into the prepared muffin cups, dividing it evenly. Bake in the oven for about 20 minutes, or until risen and golden. Cool in the tin for 10 minutes, then turn out onto a wire rack. Serve warm or cold.

RUM-GLAZED CARIBBEAN Muffins

Use your favourite tropical fruits for these muffins; pineapple, papaya and mango make a great combination.

MAKES 10

300g plain flour
2¹/₂ teaspoons baking powder
50g granulated sugar
100g soft light brown sugar
¹/₂ teaspoon salt
50g flaked coconut
150g ready-to-eat mixed dried tropical fruit, finely chopped
275ml milk
125ml vegetable oil
1 egg, lightly beaten
FOR THE ICING
100g icing sugar
1 tablespoon white rum

1. Preheat the oven to 190°C/375°F/Gas mark 5. Grease 10 cups of a 12-cup muffin tin or line 10 cups with paper muffin cases.

2. For the muffins, mix the flour, baking powder, sugars, salt, coconut and 100g of the tropical fruit in a large bowl. In a separate bowl or jug, combine the milk, vegetable oil and egg. Add the wet ingredients to the dry ingredients, mixing briefly until just combined.

3. Spoon the batter into the prepared muffin cups, dividing it evenly. Bake in the oven for about 20 minutes, or until risen and golden. Cool in the tin for 5 minutes, then turn onto a wire rack to cool completely.

4. For the icing, sift the icing sugar into a bowl and gradually blend in the rum until you have a smooth icing. Drizzle the rum icing evenly over the tops of the muffins, then scatter with the remaining chopped tropical fruit to serve.

MUFFIN TIP
If you prefer, make the icing with tropical fruit juice or orange juice instead of the rum. Flaked coconut is available from many health food shops, but use desiccated coconut if you can't find flaked coconut.

MINI ICED CHERRY
Muffins

These dainty mini muffins have a fudgy icing, coloured and
flavoured with morello cherry syrup.

MAKES 24

150g self-raising flour
3/4 teaspoon baking powder
25g butter
40g caster sugar
6 morello cherries (in a jar), drained
   and finely chopped
1 egg, lightly beaten
125ml milk
1 teaspoon vanilla extract
12 morello cherries (in a jar), drained
   and halved, to decorate

FOR THE ICING
75g icing sugar
10g unsalted butter, at room
   temperature
1 teaspoon syrup from a jar of
   morello cherries (optional)
3 teaspoons cold water

1. Preheat the oven to 190°C/375°F/Gas mark 5. Line two 12-cup mini
muffin tins or one 24-cup mini muffin tin with paper mini muffin cases.

2. For the muffins, mix the flour and baking powder in a large bowl. Rub
in the butter until the mixture resembles fine breadcrumbs. Stir in the
sugar and morello cherries. In a separate bowl or jug, mix together the
egg, milk and vanilla extract. Pour the wet mixture all at once into the dry
ingredients and mix briefly until just combined.

3. Spoon the batter into the prepared muffin cups, dividing it evenly.
Bake in the oven for about 10 minutes, or until well risen and firm to the
touch. Cool in the tins for 5 minutes, then turn out onto a wire rack.
Leave to cool completely.

4. For the icing, sift the icing sugar into a small bowl; set aside. Gently
heat the butter, cherry syrup if using and water in a small saucepan until
the butter has melted, stirring. Pour onto the icing sugar and stir until
smooth. Carefully spoon the icing over the muffins and top each with half
a morello cherry. Leave to set before serving.

RED & ORANGE Muffins

This classic combination is enhanced with chopped pecans to give a satisfying crunch and texture.

MAKES 12

300g plain flour
225g caster sugar
1 tablespoon baking powder
$\frac{1}{2}$ teaspoon salt
125g fresh or frozen cranberries
  (thawed if frozen), coarsely
  chopped
Finely grated zest of 1 orange
2 tablespoons chopped pecans
1 egg, lightly beaten
225ml milk
40g butter, melted

1. Preheat the oven to 200°C/400°F/Gas mark 6. Grease a 12-cup muffin tin or line the cups with paper muffin cases.

2. Mix the flour, sugar, baking powder and salt in a large bowl. Stir in the cranberries, orange zest and pecans.

3. In a separate bowl or jug, mix together the egg, milk and melted butter. Add the wet ingredients to the dry ingredients and mix briefly until just combined.

4. Spoon the batter into the prepared muffin cups, dividing it evenly. Bake in the oven for about 20 minutes, or until risen and golden. Cool in the tin for 10 minutes, then turn out onto a wire rack. Serve warm or cold.

MUFFIN TIP
Fresh blueberries instead of the cranberries and walnuts instead of the pecans would also work well in this recipe.

HAPPY BIRTHDAY Muffins

Lemon-flavoured muffins are split in half and sandwiched with jam. Drizzled with glacé icing, scattered with sugar sprinkles or small sweets and decorated with a birthday candle, they make a great alternative to a traditional birthday cake.

MAKES **10**

250g self-raising flour
1 teaspoon baking powder
150g caster sugar
Pinch of salt
Finely grated zest of 1 lemon
1 egg, lightly beaten
150ml milk
75g butter, melted

FOR THE FILLING & ICING

100g seedless raspberry jam
200g icing sugar
2–3 tablespoons lemon juice
Sugar strands or small sweets,
   to decorate

MUFFIN TIP

If you prefer, fill the muffins with lemon curd or chocolate spread instead of jam.

1. Preheat the oven to 190°C/375°F/Gas mark 5. Grease 10 cups of a 12-cup non-stick muffin tin.

2. For the muffins, mix the flour, baking powder, sugar, salt and lemon zest in a large bowl. In a separate bowl or jug, mix together the egg, milk and melted butter. Add the wet ingredients all at once to the dry ingredients and mix briefly until just combined.

3. Spoon the batter into the prepared muffin cups, dividing it evenly. Bake in the oven for about 20 minutes, or until well risen and golden brown. Cool in the tin for 5 minutes, then turn out onto a wire rack and leave to cool completely.

4. When the muffins are cold, split them in half horizontally, then sandwich them back together with the jam. Sift the icing sugar into a small bowl and add enough lemon juice to make a smooth, thick icing. Drizzle or spread the icing over the tops of the muffins, then decorate with sugar strands or small sweets. Leave to set before serving.

FRESH RASPBERRY & LEMON Muffins

These refreshing fresh fruit muffins have a slightly rounded rather than a peaked top and a light sponge-like texture. If lemon-flavoured yoghurt is not available, use natural yoghurt instead.

MAKES 12

300g self-raising flour
1 teaspoon bicarbonate of soda
150g caster sugar
6 tablespoons vegetable oil
150ml carton low-fat lemon-
    flavoured yoghurt
Finely grated zest and juice of
    ½ lemon
2 eggs, lightly beaten
150g fresh raspberries

1. Preheat the oven to 190°C/375°F/Gas mark 5. Grease a 12-cup muffin tin or line the cups with paper muffin cases.

2. Mix the flour, bicarbonate of soda and sugar in a large bowl. In a separate bowl or jug, mix together the vegetable oil, yoghurt, lemon zest and juice and eggs. Add the wet ingredients to the dry ingredients with the raspberries and mix briefly until just combined.

3. Spoon the batter into the prepared muffin cups, dividing it evenly. Bake in the oven for 15–18 minutes, or until risen and golden. Cool in the tin for 10 minutes, then turn out onto a wire rack. Serve warm or cold.

MUFFIN TIP
If you like, ice these muffins with a lemon glaze made from mixing together 100g sifted icing sugar and 1 tablespoon of lemon juice.

PEACH & BASIL Muffins

Use only the freshest peaches in season to get the best results. If you want to make these muffins out of season, use canned peaches in fruit juice, well-drained.

MAKES 12

2 ripe peaches, peeled, stoned and
   chopped into small dice
2 tablespoons chopped fresh basil
3 tablespoons soft light brown sugar
Grated zest and juice of ½ lemon
300g self-raising flour
½ teaspoon baking powder
50g butter
80g granulated sugar
1 egg, lightly beaten
150ml milk

1. Place the peaches in a bowl with the basil, brown sugar and lemon juice and stir to mix. Set aside to stand for about 30 minutes.

2. Preheat the oven to 200°C/400°F/Gas mark 6. Grease a 12-cup muffin tin or line the cups with paper muffin cases.

3. Mix the flour and baking powder in a large bowl, then rub in the butter until the mixture resembles fine breadcrumbs. Stir in the granulated sugar and lemon zest.

4. In a separate bowl or jug, mix together the egg and milk. Add the wet ingredients to the dry ingredients alternately with the peaches and their juices, mixing briefly until just combined.

5. Spoon the mixture into the prepared muffin cups, dividing it evenly. Bake in the oven for about 20 minutes, or until risen and golden. Cool in the tin for 10 minutes, then turn out onto a wire rack. Serve warm or cold.

MUFFIN TIP
For a tasty alternative, use fresh nectarines in place of peaches, when they are in season.

BLUEBERRY Muffins

Someone once said that "When a man grows tired of blueberry muffins, he grows tired of life". You will never tire of these delicious fruity muffins!

MAKES 12

300g self-raising flour
1 teaspoon baking powder
50g butter
80g caster sugar
150g fresh blueberries
2 eggs, lightly beaten
225ml milk
1 teaspoon vanilla extract

MUFFIN TIP
Try using fresh raspberries instead of the blueberries, and replace the vanilla extract with 1 teaspoon ground mixed spice or ground cinnamon, if you like.

1. Preheat the oven to 200°C/400°F/Gas mark 6. Grease a 12-cup muffin tin or line the cups with paper muffin cases.

2. Mix the flour and baking powder in a large bowl. Rub in the butter until the mixture resembles fine breadcrumbs. Stir the sugar and blueberries into this mixture.

3. In a separate small bowl or jug, mix together the eggs, milk and vanilla extract. Pour the egg mixture all at once into the dry ingredients and mix briefly until just combined.

4. Spoon the batter into the prepared muffin cups, dividing it evenly. Bake in the oven for about 20 minutes, or until risen and golden. Cool in the tin for 10 minutes, then turn out onto a wire rack. Serve warm or cold.

CHERRY COCONUT Muffins

Don't try using fresh cherries for this recipe – they will add too much moisture to the batter. These muffins are best made in a non-stick muffin tin, rather than with paper muffin cases.

MAKES 12

300g self-raising flour
50g soft margarine
150g glacé cherries, chopped
100g flaked coconut
1 tablespoon caster sugar
1/4 teaspoon salt
2 eggs, lightly beaten
225ml milk

MUFFIN TIP
Chopped dried cherries or chopped ready-to-eat dried apricots, used in place of the glacé cherries, would also work well in this recipe.

1. Preheat the oven to 200°C/400°F/Gas mark 6. Grease a 12-cup non-stick muffin tin.

2. Put the flour in a bowl with the margarine and blend with a fork until evenly mixed. Stir in the cherries, coconut, sugar and salt until well mixed.

3. In a separate bowl or jug, mix together the eggs and milk. Add the egg mixture to the dry ingredients and mix briefly until just combined.

4. Spoon the batter into the prepared muffin cups, dividing it evenly. Bake in the oven for 15–20 minutes, or until risen and golden. Cool in the tin for 10 minutes, then turn out onto a wire rack. Serve warm or cold.

PLUM & MARZIPAN Muffins

The marzipan softens and melts a little during the baking of these muffins and tastes fabulous with the tart, fresh plums.

MAKES 12

150g plain white flour
150g plain wholemeal flour
100g rolled oats
4 teaspoons baking powder
³/₄ teaspoon salt
50g wheat bran
150g soft light brown sugar
250g unpeeled stoned plums, chopped
175ml unsweetened orange juice
125ml vegetable oil
2 eggs, lightly beaten
Finely grated zest of ¹/₂ orange
100g marzipan, cut into small cubes
25g flaked almonds

1. Preheat the oven to 180°C/350°F/Gas mark 4. Grease a 12-cup muffin tin or line the cups with paper muffin cases.

2. Mix the flours, oats, baking powder, salt, wheat bran and sugar in a large bowl. In a separate bowl or jug, mix together the plums, orange juice, vegetable oil, eggs and orange zest.

3. Add the wet ingredients to the dry ingredients along with the marzipan and flaked almonds and mix briefly until just combined.

4. Spoon the batter into the prepared muffin cups, dividing it evenly. Bake in the oven for 25–30 minutes, or until risen and golden. Cool in the tin for 10 minutes, then turn out onto a wire rack. Serve warm or cold.

BANOFFEE Muffins

These moist banana muffins with their rich toffee-fudge sauce are absolutely delicious served warm. They are best made in a non-stick muffin tin, rather than with paper muffin cases.

MAKES 12

300g self-raising flour
1/2 teaspoon baking powder
1 teaspoon bicarbonate of soda
1/2 teaspoon ground mixed spice
1/2 teaspoon salt
3 large well-ripened bananas, about
   450g unpeeled weight
110g caster sugar
1 egg, lightly beaten
6 tablespoons milk
75g butter, melted
1 teaspoon vanilla extract

FOR THE TOFFEE-FUDGE SAUCE
50g butter
75g soft light brown sugar
50g caster sugar
150g golden syrup
125ml double cream
1 tablespoon lemon juice
1 teaspoon vanilla extract

1. Preheat the oven to 190°C/375°F/Gas mark 5. Grease a 12-cup non-stick muffin tin.

2. For the muffins, mix the flour, baking powder, bicarbonate of soda, mixed spice and salt in a large bowl. In a separate bowl, mash the peeled bananas thoroughly with a potato masher or fork until puréed. Stir in the sugar, egg, milk, melted butter and vanilla extract. Add the wet ingredients to the dry ingredients and mix briefly until just combined.

3. Spoon the batter into the prepared muffin cups, dividing it evenly. Bake in the oven for 18–20 minutes, or until well risen, golden and firm to the touch. Cool in the tin for 5 minutes, then turn out onto a wire rack.

4. For the toffee-fudge sauce, melt the butter, sugars and golden syrup in a medium heavy-based saucepan over a very low heat. Cook gently, stirring frequently for 5 minutes. Remove the pan from the heat and slowly stir in the cream, lemon juice and vanilla extract. Pour the sauce over the muffins and serve warm.

BLUEBERRY
BUTTERMILK Muffins

If using frozen blueberries, thaw them thoroughly and pat dry
on kitchen paper before tossing in icing sugar.

MAKES 12

150g fresh or frozen blueberries
25g icing sugar
300g plain flour
2 teaspoons baking powder
Pinch of salt
150g soft light brown sugar
1 egg, lightly beaten
225ml buttermilk
2 tablespoons milk
50g butter, melted
Finely grated zest of ½ orange

1. Preheat the oven to 200°C/400°F/Gas mark 6. Grease a 12-cup muffin tin or line the cups with paper muffin cases.

2. Put the blueberries into a large bowl. Sift over the icing sugar and toss the blueberries in the sugar to coat. Add the flour, baking powder, salt and brown sugar, then stir together.

3. In a separate bowl or jug, mix together the egg, buttermilk, milk, melted butter and orange zest. Add the buttermilk mixture all at once to the dry ingredients and mix briefly until just combined.

4. Spoon the batter into the prepared muffin cups, dividing it evenly. Bake in the oven for 18–20 minutes, or until risen and golden. Cool in the tin for 5 minutes, then turn out onto a wire rack. Serve warm or cold.

MUFFIN TIP
*Instead of butter, you
can use 4 tablespoons
of sunflower oil,
if you prefer.*

APPLE STREUSEL Muffins

These moist muffins are studded with fresh chunks of apple and juicy sultanas.
A grated streusel topping adds a lovely crunchy texture.

MAKES 12

250g plain flour
2$\frac{1}{2}$ teaspoons baking powder
1$\frac{1}{2}$ teaspoons ground cinnamon
1 teaspoon ground ginger
Pinch of freshly grated nutmeg
$\frac{1}{2}$ teaspoon salt
150g caster sugar
1 egg, lightly beaten
150ml milk
6 tablespoons vegetable oil
50g sultanas
3 medium eating apples (about 225g
　　whole/unprepared weight), peeled,
　　cored and chopped

FOR THE TOPPING
50g plain flour
40g butter
2 tablespoons soft light brown sugar

1. Preheat the oven to 190°C/375°F/Gas mark 5. Grease a 12-cup muffin tin or line the cups with paper muffin cases.

2. For the topping, sift the flour into a bowl. Cut the butter into small pieces and rub into the flour until the mixture resembles fine breadcrumbs. Stir in the sugar, then gather the dough together and gently squeeze it into a ball. Coarsely grate the dough and set aside.

3. For the muffins, mix the flour, baking powder, cinnamon, ginger, nutmeg, salt and sugar in a large bowl. In a separate bowl, mix together the egg, milk, vegetable oil, sultanas and chopped apples. Add the apple mixture all at once to the dry ingredients and mix briefly until just combined.

4. Spoon the batter into the prepared muffin cups, dividing it evenly, then sprinkle the tops with the grated topping.
Bake in the oven for about 20 minutes, or until risen and golden. Cool in the tin for 10 minutes, then turn out onto a wire rack. Serve warm or cold.

MUFFIN TIP
If time allows, wrap and chill the streusel dough in the fridge for 15 minutes to make it easier to grate.

CLEMENTINE Muffins

If fresh clementines are not available, substitute a small (227g) can of mandarin segments, well drained and chopped.

MAKES 12

300g plain flour
2 teaspoons baking powder
1/2 teaspoon salt
1/4 teaspoon ground allspice
1/4 teaspoon freshly grated nutmeg
125g caster sugar
60g margarine or butter
1 egg, lightly beaten
200ml milk
3 clementines or mandarin oranges, peeled, broken into segments and chopped

FOR THE TOPPING (OPTIONAL)
65g caster sugar
1/2 teaspoon ground cinnamon
50g butter, melted

1. Preheat the oven to 180°C/350°F/Gas mark 4. Grease a 12-cup muffin tin or line the cups with paper muffin cases.

2. For the muffins, mix the flour, baking powder, salt, allspice, nutmeg and sugar in a large bowl. Rub in the margarine or butter until the mixture resembles fine breadcrumbs.

3. In a separate bowl or jug, mix together the egg and milk, then add the egg mixture all at once to the dry ingredients. Mix briefly until just combined, then fold in the clementine or mandarin pieces.

4. Spoon the batter into the prepared muffin cups, dividing it evenly. Bake in the oven for 20–25 minutes, or until risen and golden.

5. Meanwhile, for the topping, mix together the sugar and cinnamon in a small bowl and set aside. Remove the baked muffins from the tin while still warm. Dip the tops of the muffins in melted butter, then dip them in the cinnamon sugar. Transfer to a wire rack and allow to cool for 10 minutes before serving. Serve warm or cold.

SOUR CHERRY Muffins filled with Jam

If you don't have any fresh cherries, use canned or bottled stoned cherries for this recipe. Make sure they are well drained.

MAKES 12

300g plain flour
1 teaspoon baking powder
1/2 teaspoon bicarbonate of soda
1/2 teaspoon salt
1/2 teaspoon ground cardamom
125g caster sugar
150g fresh cherries, stoned and
    coarsely chopped
50g butter, melted
1 egg, lightly beaten
225ml soured cream
1/2 teaspoon vanilla extract
3–4 tablespoons sour cherry jam
3 tablespoons flaked almonds

1. Preheat the oven to 200°C/400°F/Gas mark 6. Grease a 12-cup muffin tin or line the cups with paper muffin cases.

2. Mix the flour, baking powder, bicarbonate of soda, salt and cardamom in a large bowl. Stir in the sugar and cherries and mix well.

3. In a separate bowl, beat together the melted butter, egg, soured cream and vanilla extract. Pour the wet ingredients into the flour mixture and mix briefly until just combined.

4. Spoon half of the batter evenly into the prepared muffin cups. Add about 1 teaspoon of jam to each, then top with the remaining batter, dividing it evenly. Sprinkle the tops with the flaked almonds.

5. Bake in the oven for about 20 minutes, or until risen and golden Cool in the tin for 10 minutes, then turn out onto a wire rack. Serve warm or cold.

TROPICAL FRUIT Muffins with Passion Fruit Glaze

Fresh mango, pineapple and flaked coconut add delicious flavour to these passion fruit-glazed muffins.

MAKES 12

1 small very ripe mango, peeled and
    stoned
300g plain flour
4 teaspoons baking powder
¹/₂ teaspoon salt
225g caster sugar
50g flaked coconut
50ml vegetable oil
225ml milk
1 egg, lightly beaten
225g canned crushed pineapple in
    juice, drained
FOR THE PASSION FRUIT GLAZE
4 ripe passion fruit
4 tablespoons granulated sugar

1. Preheat the oven to 200°C/400°F/Gas mark 6. Grease a 12-cup muffin tin or line the cups with paper muffin cases. Purée the mango flesh in a blender or food processor. Set aside.

2. Mix the flour, baking powder, salt and caster sugar in a large bowl. Stir in the coconut. In a separate bowl, mix together the vegetable oil, milk and egg. Add the wet ingredients to the dry ingredients and mix briefly until just combined. Fold in the mango purée and drained pineapple.

3. Spoon the batter into the prepared muffin cups, dividing it evenly. Bake in the oven for 15–18 minutes, or until risen and golden.

4. Meanwhile, for the passion fruit glaze, cut each passion fruit in half and scoop out the flesh and juice, then press the pulp through a sieve into a small saucepan. Discard the pips. Add the granulated sugar to the pan and stir over a low heat until the sugar has dissolved. Increase the heat and bring the mixture to the boil, then boil for 3 minutes or until syrupy. Remove the pan from the heat.

5. Spoon the passion fruit syrup over the muffins while they are still hot. Allow them to cool slightly in the tin. Serve warm or just cooled.

CARROT, APPLE & COCONUT Muffins

This is an unusual combination that makes very moist muffins. Dried apple is readily available from health food stores and many large supermarkets.

MAKES 12

150g plain wholemeal flour
150g plain white flour
175g caster sugar
2 teaspoons baking powder
1 teaspoon ground cinnamon
½ teaspoon bicarbonate of soda
200g carrot, finely grated
100g dried apple, chopped
75g raisins
50g walnuts, chopped
50g flaked coconut
2 eggs, lightly beaten
125ml buttermilk
125ml milk
2 teaspoons vanilla extract

1. Preheat the oven to 180°C/350°F/Gas mark 4. Grease a 12-cup muffin tin or line the cups with paper muffin cases.

2. Mix the flours, sugar, baking powder, cinnamon and bicarbonate of soda in a large bowl. Stir in the carrot, apple, raisins, walnuts and coconut.

3. In a separate bowl, mix together the eggs, buttermilk, milk and vanilla extract. Add the wet ingredients all at once to the dry ingredients and mix briefly until just combined. Carefully spoon the batter into the prepared muffin cups, dividing it evenly.

4. Bake in the oven for 20–25 minutes, or until risen and golden. Cool in the tin for 10 minutes, then turn out onto a wire rack. Serve warm or cold.

MUFFIN TIP
Try dried pear instead of the apple in this recipe if you prefer.

PEACH UPSIDE-DOWN Muffins

These muffins are best made in a non-stick muffin tin, rather than with paper muffin cases.

MAKES 12

60g cold butter, cut into 12 pieces
100g soft light brown sugar
400g can peach slices in fruit juice, drained
200g plain flour
225g caster sugar
2 teaspoons baking powder
½ teaspoon salt
2 eggs, lightly beaten
150ml soured cream
25g white vegetable margarine, melted

1. Preheat the oven to 190°C/375°F/Gas mark 5. Grease a 12-cup non-stick muffin tin.

2. Divide the butter and brown sugar evenly between the cups of the prepared tin. Place in the oven for about 5 minutes, or until the butter and sugar have melted. Remove from the oven and arrange the peach slices in the bottoms of the muffin cups.

3. Meanwhile, mix the flour, caster sugar, baking powder and salt in a large bowl. In a separate bowl, mix together the eggs, soured cream and melted margarine. Add the wet ingredients all at once to the dry ingredients and mix briefly until just combined.

4. Spoon the batter on top of the peach slices in the muffin cups, dividing it evenly. Bake in the oven for 20–25 minutes, or until risen and golden. Cool in the tin for about 10 minutes, then invert the muffins onto a plate or platter. Serve warm.

MUFFIN TIP
Use chopped canned pineapple, drained, in place of peach slices, if you prefer.

SOURED CREAM & SULTANA

Muffins with Cinnamon Honey Butter

Briefly soaking the sultanas in hot water makes them plump and juicy and ensures the muffins remain moist.

MAKES 12

150g sultanas
225ml boiling water
375g self-raising flour
1 teaspoon baking powder
200g caster sugar
Finely grated zest of 1 lemon
175ml soured cream
125ml milk
2 eggs, lightly beaten
FOR THE CINNAMON HONEY BUTTER
125g butter, softened
1 teaspoon ground cinnamon
1 tablespoon clear honey
100g icing sugar, sifted

1. Preheat the oven to 190°C/375°F/Gas mark 5. Grease a 12-cup muffin tin or line the cups with paper muffin cases.

2. For the muffins, put the sultanas in a bowl and pour over the boiling water. Leave to soak for 10 minutes, then drain well.

3. Meanwhile, mix the flour, baking powder, sugar and lemon zest in a large bowl. In a separate bowl or jug, mix together the soured cream, milk, eggs and soaked sultanas. Add the soured cream mixture to the dry ingredients, mixing briefly until just combined.

4. Spoon the batter into the prepared muffin cups, dividing it evenly. Bake in the oven for about 20 minutes, or until risen and golden. Cool in the tin for 5 minutes, then turn out onto a wire rack.

5. For the cinnamon honey butter, in a bowl, beat together the butter, cinnamon and honey. Gradually beat in the icing sugar until the mixture is pale and fluffy. Serve the muffins warm or cold with the butter.

PINEAPPLE COCONUT Muffins

Like a pina colada without the rum, these muffins owe their moist texture to the combination of rich pineapple and coconut – a little delicious taste of the tropics in one bite!

MAKES 12

300g plain flour
4 teaspoons baking powder
$\frac{1}{2}$ teaspoon salt
225g caster sugar
50g fresh coconut flesh, grated
50ml vegetable oil
225ml milk
1 egg, lightly beaten
150g canned crushed pineapple in juice, drained

1. Preheat the oven to 200°C/400°F/Gas mark 6. Grease a 12-cup muffin tin or line the cups with paper muffin cases.

2. Mix the flour, baking powder, salt and sugar in a large bowl. Stir in the coconut. In a separate bowl, mix together the vegetable oil, milk and egg. Add the wet ingredients to the dry ingredients and mix briefly until just combined, then stir in the drained pineapple.

3. Spoon the batter into the prepared muffin cups, dividing it evenly. Bake in the oven for 15–18 minutes, or until risen and golden. Cool in the tin for 10 minutes, then turn out onto a wire rack. Serve warm or cold.

MUFFIN TIP
If you can't buy fresh coconut, use flaked or desiccated coconut instead.

LIME & FRESH COCONUT
Muffins

Fresh coconuts are not difficult to deal with, but you must drain the coconut water before cracking them open completely. Using a metal skewer, punch a hole in two of the three "eyes" at one end and drain the coconut water out. Bash the coconut as hard as you can with a hammer to open, then remove the flesh before grating.

MAKES 12

100g fresh coconut flesh, grated
300g self-raising flour
225g caster sugar
Finely grated zest and juice of 3 limes
1 egg, lightly beaten
225ml milk
60g butter, melted

1. Preheat the oven to 200°C/400°F/Gas mark 6. Grease a 12-cup muffin tin or line the cups with paper muffin cases.

2. Set aside about 3 tablespoons of the coconut. Mix the flour and sugar in a large bowl. Add the remaining coconut and the lime zest and mix well.

3. In a separate bowl, mix together the lime juice, egg, milk and melted butter. Add the wet ingredients to the dry ingredients and mix briefly until just combined.

4. Spoon the batter into the prepared muffin cups, dividing it evenly, then sprinkle the tops with the reserved coconut. Bake in the oven for about 20 minutes, or until risen and golden. Cool in the tin for 10 minutes, then turn out onto a wire rack. Serve warm or cold.

DRIED CHERRY, APPLE & PECAN Muffins

If dried cherries are not available, try making these delicious fruit and nut muffins with dried cranberries instead.

MAKES 12

300g plain flour
225g caster sugar
1 tablespoon baking powder
$\frac{1}{2}$ teaspoon salt
1 large eating apple, cored and
   coarsely chopped (leave skin on)
150g dried cherries, coarsely chopped
75g pecans, chopped
2 eggs, lightly beaten
125g butter, melted
175ml buttermilk
3 tablespoons demerara sugar
1 teaspoon ground cinnamon

1. Preheat the oven to 200°C/400°F/Gas mark 6. Grease a 12-cup muffin tin or line the cups with paper muffin cases.

2. Mix the flour, caster sugar, baking powder and salt in a large bowl. Stir in the apple, cherries and pecans.

3. In a separate bowl, mix together the eggs, melted butter and buttermilk. Add the egg mixture all at once to the dry ingredients and mix briefly until just combined.

4. Spoon the batter into the prepared muffins cups, dividing it evenly. Combine the demerara sugar and cinnamon and sprinkle evenly over the muffins. Bake in the oven for about 20 minutes, or until risen and golden. Cool in the tin for 10 minutes, then turn out onto a wire rack. Serve warm or cold.

MUFFIN TIP
Try changing the nuts in this recipe for a different flavour. You could substitute the pecans for almonds or walnuts for example.

STRAWBERRIES & CREAM
Muffins

These vanilla-flavoured muffins are filled with strawberry conserve and topped with whipped cream and fresh strawberries.

MAKES 10

250g plain flour
1 tablespoon baking powder
Pinch of salt
150g caster sugar
1 egg, lightly beaten
225ml milk
85g butter, melted
2 teaspoons vanilla extract
100g strawberry conserve
150ml whipping or double cream
2 teaspoons icing sugar
Small or medium strawberries,
    halved, to decorate

1. Preheat the oven to 190°C/375°F/Gas mark 5. Grease 10 cups of a 12-cup non-stick muffin tin.

2. Mix the flour, baking powder, salt and caster sugar in a large bowl. In a separate bowl or jug, mix together the egg, milk, melted butter and vanilla extract. Add the milk mixture all at once to the dry ingredients and mix briefly until just combined.

3. Spoon the batter into the prepared muffin cups, dividing it evenly. Bake in the oven for about 20 minutes, or until risen and golden. Cool in the tin for 10 minutes, then turn out onto a wire rack and leave to cool completely.

4. When the muffins are cold, cut each one in half horizontally. Spread strawberry conserve on the bottom half of each muffin and replace the top half.

5. Whip the cream with the icing sugar in a small bowl until soft peaks form. Either spoon or pipe a swirl of cream on top of each muffin. Arrange the strawberry halves on top of the muffins. Chill until ready to serve.

LEMON POPPY SEED Muffins

It's best to make these muffins in a non-stick muffin tin without paper muffin cases so that the syrup can soak into the muffins without running under the paper.

MAKES 12

Finely grated zest and juice
  of 2 lemons
225g caster sugar
300g self-raising flour
2 tablespoons poppy seeds
1 egg, lightly beaten
225ml milk
60g butter, melted
FOR THE LEMON SYRUP
100g icing sugar, sifted
Juice of 1 lemon

1. Preheat the oven to 200°C/400°F/Gas mark 6. Grease a 12-cup non-stick muffin tin.

2. For the muffins, mix 2 teaspoons of the lemon zest and 2 tablespoons of the sugar in a small bowl. Set aside.

3. Mix the flour, poppy seeds and remaining sugar in a large bowl. In a separate bowl or jug, mix together the remaining lemon zest, the lemon juice, egg, milk and melted butter. Add this to the flour and sugar mixture and stir until just combined.

4. Spoon the batter into the prepared muffin cups, dividing it evenly, then sprinkle the tops with the reserved sugar and lemon zest mixture. Bake in the oven for about 20 minutes, or until risen and golden.

5. Meanwhile, for the lemon syrup, mix the icing sugar and lemon juice in a bowl until smooth and well blended. Spoon the lemon syrup over the hot baked muffins, then let them cool in the tin. Turn out and serve cold.

PINEAPPLE & PASSION FRUIT Muffins

MAKES **10**

4 ripe passion fruit
225g can crushed pineapple in fruit
　juice
About 5 tablespoons unsweetened
　pineapple or orange juice
300g self-raising flour
1 teaspoon baking powder
$\frac{1}{4}$ teaspoon bicarbonate of soda
$\frac{1}{4}$ teaspoon salt
110g caster sugar
1 egg, lightly beaten
6 tablespoons vegetable oil
FOR THE PASSION FRUIT TOPPING
60g butter, softened
100g icing sugar, sifted
Toasted coconut flakes, for sprinkling

MUFFIN TIP
*Make sure that the
passion fruit are really
ripe before extracting the
juice; their skins should
be very wrinkly
and dimpled*

1. Preheat the oven to 190°C/375°F/Gas mark 5. Grease 10 cups of a 12-cup muffin tin or line 10 cups with paper muffin cases.

2. For the muffins, halve the passion fruit and scoop out the flesh and juice into a fine sieve placed over a jug. Press the pulp with the back of a spoon to squeeze out all the juice. Discard the pips. Reserve 1 tablespoon of the juice for the icing. Tip the pineapple into the sieve and press out most of the juice. Measure the juice in the jug and make up to 225ml with the pineapple or orange juice. Set aside.

3. Mix the flour, baking powder, bicarbonate of soda, salt and sugar in a large bowl. Stir the egg, vegetable oil and crushed pineapple into the fruit juice in the jug. Add the pineapple mixture all at once to the dry ingredients and mix briefly until just combined.

4. Spoon the batter into the prepared muffin cups, dividing evenly. Bake in the oven for about 20 minutes, or until risen and golden. Cool in the tin for 10 minutes, then turn onto a wire rack and leave to cool completely.

5. For the passion fruit topping, beat the butter in a bowl until creamy. Gradually beat in two-thirds of the icing sugar. Beat in the reserved passion fruit juice, then add the rest of the icing sugar, beating until the mixture is light and fluffy. Spread a little of the topping mixture over the top of each muffin and sprinkle with toasted coconut flakes to serve.

BUTTERY APPLE CUSTARD Muffins

Here the apples are gently cooked in butter until tender, then tossed in ground cinnamon. A small amount of custard powder lightens the mixture and gives it a subtle golden colour.

MAKES 12

125g butter, melted
2 eating apples, peeled, cored and finely chopped
1½ teaspoons ground cinnamon
250g plain flour
50g custard powder
225g caster sugar
1 tablespoon baking powder
½ teaspoon salt
2 eggs, lightly beaten
175ml buttermilk
2 tablespoons demerara sugar

MUFFIN TIP
If you haven't got any custard powder, use cornflour instead. It will give the same light texture, but won't add any colour to the muffins.

1. Preheat the oven to 200°C/400°F/Gas mark 6. Grease a 12-cup muffin tin or line the cups with paper muffin cases.

2. Pour about half of the melted butter into a heavy-based non-stick saucepan. Add the apples and cook gently for 10 minutes, or until very tender. Sprinkle over the cinnamon and stir in. Remove the pan from the heat and set aside to cool for 5 minutes.

3. Mix the flour, custard powder, caster sugar, baking powder and salt in a large bowl. In a separate bowl or jug, mix together the eggs, buttermilk, remaining melted butter and apple mixture. Add the wet ingredients to the dry ingredients, and mix briefly until just combined.

4. Spoon the batter into the prepared muffin cups, dividing it evenly. Sprinkle the demerara sugar evenly over the tops of the muffins. Bake in the oven for about 20 minutes, or until risen and golden. Cool in the tin for 10 minutes, then turn out onto a wire rack. Serve warm or cold.

SUGAR-CRUSTED CITRUS Muffins

These light lemon and lime muffins have a tangy topping that separates into a sticky syrup and a crunchy sugary crust.

MAKES 10

250g self-raising flour
1 teaspoon baking powder
$\frac{1}{2}$ teaspoon salt
110g caster sugar
225ml milk
Finely grated zest of $\frac{1}{2}$ lemon
Finely grated zest of $\frac{1}{2}$ lime
1 egg, lightly beaten
75g butter, melted

FOR THE CRUNCHY TOPPING
110g granulated sugar
Juice of 1 small lemon
Thinly pared strips of rind of $\frac{1}{2}$ lemon
Thinly pared strips of rind of $\frac{1}{2}$ lime

1. Preheat the oven to 190°C/375°F/Gas mark 5. Grease 10 cups of a 12-cup muffin tin or line 10 cups with paper muffin cases.

2. For the muffins, mix the flour, baking powder, salt and sugar in a large bowl. Pour the milk into a jug. Stir in the lemon and lime zest, egg and melted butter. Add the wet ingredients to the dry ingredients and mix briefly until just combined.

3. Spoon the batter into the prepared muffin cups, dividing it evenly. Bake in the oven for about 20 minutes, or until risen and golden. Remove from the oven and leave the baked muffins in the tin.

4. While the muffins are baking, make the crunchy topping. Mix the sugar and lemon juice in a bowl until blended. Stir in the thinly pared strips of lemon and lime rind. When the muffins come out of the oven, spoon the citrus mixture over the hot muffins. Leave to cool in the tin, then turn out and serve.

MUFFIN TIP
Make sure you use granulated and not caster sugar for the topping.

JAM-FILLED MINI Muffins

You can use this recipe to make 12 regular-sized muffins if you prefer a larger treat.

MAKES 36

250g self-raising flour
1 teaspoon baking powder
50g butter
80g caster sugar
2 eggs, lightly beaten
225ml milk
1 teaspoon vanilla extract
5–6 tablespoons raspberry or
    strawberry jam
FOR THE TOPPING
50g butter
1 teaspoon ground cinnamon
50g granulated sugar

1. Preheat the oven to 200°C/400°F/Gas mark 6. Grease three 12-cup mini muffin tins or one 24-cup mini muffin tin and one 12-cup mini muffin tin, or line the cups with paper mini muffin cases.

2. For the muffins, mix the flour and baking powder in a large bowl. Rub in the butter until the mixture resembles fine breadcrumbs. Stir in the sugar.

3. In a separate small bowl, mix together the eggs, milk and vanilla extract, then pour the milk mixture all at once into the dry ingredients and mix briefly until just combined.

4. Put a small spoonful of the mixture into each prepared muffin cup. Add about ½ teaspoon of jam to each, then top with the remaining muffin batter, dividing it evenly. Bake in the oven for 8–10 minutes, or until well risen, golden and firm to the touch. Cool in the tin for a few minutes, then turn out onto a wire rack.

5. For the topping, melt the butter in a small saucepan over a low heat, then remove the pan from the heat. In a small bowl, mix together the cinnamon and sugar. Brush each baked warm mini muffin all over with a little melted butter, then roll in the cinnamon sugar. Set aside to cool. Serve warm or cold.

CHRISTMAS Muffins

Incredibly quick and simple to make, these are a great alternative to mince pies during the festive period.

MAKES 10

300g self-raising flour
1 teaspoon baking powder
1 teaspoon ground mixed spice
100g soft light brown sugar
175g mincemeat
1 egg, lightly beaten
100g butter, melted
175ml buttermilk
1 tablespoon milk
2 teaspoons demerara sugar

1. Preheat the oven to 200°C/400°F/Gas mark 6. Grease 10 cups of a 12-cup muffin tin or line 10 cups with paper muffin cases.

2. Mix the flour, baking powder, mixed spice and brown sugar in a large bowl. In a separate bowl or jug, mix together the mincemeat, egg, melted butter, buttermilk and milk. Add the wet ingredients to the dry ingredients and mix briefly until just combined.

3. Spoon the batter into the prepared muffin cups, dividing it evenly, then sprinkle the tops with demerara sugar. Bake in the oven for 18–20 minutes, or until risen and golden. Cool in the tin for 10 minutes, then turn out onto a wire rack. Serve warm or cold.

MUFFIN TIP
Choose a 'luxury' type of mincemeat for these muffins, or add a few chopped glacé cherries and nuts to the mixture and substitute brandy for the milk.

RED, WHITE & BLUE Muffins

Don't overdo the red and blue icing on these muffins; a subtle finish looks much more tempting.

MUFFIN TIP
If preferred, drizzle melted white chocolate on top of the muffins and scatter with chopped dried blueberries and cherries.

MAKES 12

300g plain flour
2¹/₂ teaspoons baking powder
125g caster sugar
¹/₂ teaspoon salt
75g dried cherries
75g dried blueberries
100g macadamia nuts, roughly chopped
225ml milk
125ml vegetable oil
1 egg, lightly beaten
FOR THE ICING
100g icing sugar
1 tablespoon warm water
Red and blue food colouring

1. Preheat the oven to 190°C/375°F/Gas mark 5. Grease a 12-cup muffin tin or line the cups with paper muffin cases.

2. For the muffins, mix the flour, baking powder, sugar, salt, dried cherries and blueberries and macadamia nuts in a large bowl. In a separate bowl or jug, mix together the milk, vegetable oil and egg. Add the wet ingredients to the dry ingredients, mixing briefly until just combined.

3. Spoon the batter into the prepared muffin cups, dividing it evenly. Bake in the oven for about 18–20 minutes, or until risen and golden. Cool in the tin for 5 minutes, then turn onto a wire rack and leave to cool completely.

4. For the icing, sift the icing sugar into a bowl and gradually blend in the water until you have a smooth icing. Colour about a quarter of the icing red and a quarter blue, leaving half the icing white. Spread the white icing on top of all the muffins and leave to set. Fill two small piping bags with the red and blue icing and drizzle stripes and spots over the white iced muffins. Leave the icing to set before serving.

CLEMENTINE & CRANBERRY Muffins

MAKES 12

3 small clementines, about 150g in
    total weight
175ml water
300g plain flour
1½ teaspoons baking powder
½ teaspoon bicarbonate of soda
125g caster sugar
½ teaspoon salt
150g dried cranberries
1 egg, lightly beaten
85g butter, melted

FOR THE TOPPING

50g rolled oats
50g soft light brown sugar
25g plain flour
1 teaspoon ground cinnamon
60g butter, cut into small pieces

1. Roughly chop the clementines (leaving their peel on), remove any pips, then put the clementines in a small saucepan with the water. Bring to the boil, then reduce the heat, half-cover the pan with a lid and simmer for 20 minutes, until really tender. Remove the pan from the heat and leave to cool for 10 minutes, then purée the mixture in a blender or food processor until smooth. Set aside.

2. Preheat the oven to 190°C/375°F/Gas mark 5. Grease a 12-cup muffin tin or line the cups with paper muffin cases.

3. Make the topping by placing all the ingredients in a bowl and rubbing in the butter. Alternatively, put all the ingredients in a food processor and process until lumps form. Set aside.

4. For the muffins, mix the flour, baking powder, bicarbonate of soda, sugar, salt and cranberries in a large bowl. Measure the clementine purée in a jug and make up to 225ml with water if needed. Stir in the egg and melted butter. Add to the dry ingredients and mix briefly until just combined.

5. Spoon the batter into the prepared muffin cups, dividing it evenly, then sprinkle the topping mixture evenly over the tops of the muffins. Bake in the oven for 18–20 minutes, or until well risen and golden. Cool in the tin for 5 minutes, then turn out onto a wire rack. Serve warm or cold.

MINI CONFETTI
Muffins

Decorate these tiny muffins with a selection of pretty icings in the colour theme of a wedding or christening party.

MAKES 24

150g self-raising flour
½ teaspoon baking powder
50g caster sugar
40g mixed glacé fruit, very
    finely chopped
3 tablespoons vegetable oil
Finely grated zest of ½ small orange
1 tablespoon unsweetened
    orange juice
5 tablespoons low-fat natural
    yoghurt
1 egg, lightly beaten

FOR THE ICING
100g icing sugar
1 tablespoon warm water
A few drops of several different food
    colourings of your choice
Confetti-type sugar sprinkles,
    to decorate

1. Preheat the oven to 190°C/375°F/Gas mark 5. Grease two 12-cup mini muffin tins or one 24-cup mini muffin tin, or line the cups with paper mini muffin cases.

2. For the muffins, mix the flour, baking powder, sugar and glacé fruit in a medium bowl. In a separate bowl or jug, mix together the vegetable oil, orange zest, orange juice, yoghurt and egg. Add the wet ingredients to the dry ingredients and mix briefly until just combined.

3. Spoon the batter into the prepared muffin cups, dividing it evenly. Bake in the oven for 10–12 minutes, or until well risen and firm to the touch. Cool in the tins for 5 minutes, then turn out onto a wire rack and leave to cool completely.

4. For the icing, sift the icing sugar into a mixing bowl, add the water and blend until smooth. Divide the icing into two or three small bowls and add a drop or two of food colouring to each to achieve the desired colours. Mix well, then spoon a little icing on top of each mini muffin and scatter with a few sugar sprinkles. Leave to set before serving.

EASTER Muffins

MAKES 10

150g self-raising flour
1/2 teaspoon bicarbonate of soda
80g caster sugar
60g butter, melted
5 tablespoons low-fat lemon-
   flavoured yoghurt
Finely grated zest of 1/2 lemon
1 tablespoon lemon juice
1 egg, lightly beaten

FOR THE LIME SYRUP
Finely grated zest and juice of 1 lime
25g caster sugar

FOR THE ICING
250g icing sugar
25g butter, melted
3 tablespoons lemon juice
Yellow and green food colouring
30 mini sugar-coated Easter eggs

1. Preheat the oven to 190°C/375°F/Gas mark 5. Line 10 cups of a 12-cup muffin tin with paper muffin cases.

2. For the muffins, mix the flour, bicarbonate of soda and sugar in a large bowl. In a separate bowl or jug, mix together the melted butter, yoghurt, lemon zest, lemon juice and egg. Add the wet ingredients to the dry ingredients and mix briefly until just combined.

3. Spoon the batter into the prepared muffin cups, dividing it evenly. Bake in the oven for about 15 minutes, or until risen and golden.

4. While the muffins are baking, make the lime syrup. Gently heat the lime zest and juice and sugar in a small saucepan until the sugar has dissolved. Remove the pan from the heat and leave to cool for 5 minutes, then pour the syrup through a fine sieve into a jug. Drizzle a little of the warm syrup over each hot baked muffin. Leave to cool completely in the tin.

5. For the icing, sift the icing sugar into a mixing bowl. Gently heat the butter and lemon juice in a small saucepan until melted. Pour the melted mixture over the icing sugar and stir until smooth and glossy.

6. Spoon half of the icing into a separate bowl. Add two drops of yellow colouring to one icing and a drop of green colouring to the other. Stir until blended, then use the icings to decorate five of the cold muffins pale yellow and five pale green. Decorate each muffin with a cluster of three mini Easter eggs. Leave to set before serving.

NUT & SPICE
MUFFINS

MOIST ALMOND & PEAR Muffins

Pears and almonds have a natural affinity, as shown in these moreish muffins.

MAKES 12

300g plain flour
1 tablespoon baking powder
1/4 teaspoon freshly grated nutmeg
4 tablespoons ground almonds
100g blanched almonds, chopped
100g marzipan, chopped into
    small pieces
150g soft light brown sugar
1 egg, lightly beaten
200ml unsweetened pear or
    apple juice
75g butter, melted
2 small ripe pears, peeled, cored
    and chopped
25g flaked almonds
1 teaspoon icing sugar

1. Preheat the oven to 190°C/375°F/Gas mark 5. Grease a 12-cup muffin tin or line the cups with paper muffin cases.

2. Mix the flour, baking powder, nutmeg, ground and chopped almonds, marzipan and brown sugar in a large bowl. In a separate bowl or jug, mix together the egg, pear or apple juice, melted butter and pears. Add the pear mixture all at once to the dry ingredients and mix briefly until just combined.

3. Spoon the batter into the prepared muffin cups, dividing it evenly, then sprinkle the tops with flaked almonds. Bake in the oven for 18-20 minutes, or until well risen and golden.

4. Cool in the tin for 5 minutes, then turn out onto a wire rack. Dust the tops with sifted icing sugar and serve warm or cold.

MUFFIN TIP
If available, use toasted blanched almonds for a more distinctive nutty flavour.

CARAMEL ORANGE
Muffins

MAKES 12

1 large orange, peeled
125g granulated sugar
2 tablespoons water
340g self-raising flour
1 teaspoon baking powder
$\frac{1}{2}$ teaspoon ground cinnamon
$\frac{1}{4}$ teaspoon ground cloves
$\frac{1}{4}$ teaspoon ground allspice
Pinch of salt
50g butter
80g caster sugar
65g pistachio nuts, chopped
2 eggs, lightly beaten
225ml milk

1. Preheat the oven to 200°C/400°F/Gas mark 6. Grease a 12-cup muffin tin or line the cups with paper muffin cases.

2. Working over a bowl to collect any juice, cut the orange into segments, then coarsely chop them and add to the bowl. Set aside.

3. Combine the granulated sugar and water in a small, heavy-based saucepan and stir over a low heat until the sugar has dissolved. Increase the heat and bring the sugar mixture to the boil. Boil for about 7–10 minutes, or until the mixture has turned a dark caramel colour.

4. Remove the pan from the heat and carefully add the chopped orange flesh and all its juice. Be careful: the mixture will bubble fiercely. Allow the mixture to cool, then drain the oranges, reserving 175ml of the syrup.

5. Mix the flour, baking powder, cinnamon, cloves, allspice and salt in a large bowl. Rub in the butter until the mixture resembles fine breadcrumbs, then stir in the caster sugar and pistachio nuts, mixing well.

6. In a separate small bowl or jug, mix together the eggs and milk, then pour into the dry ingredients. Add the drained oranges and mix until just combined. Spoon the batter into the muffin cups, dividing it evenly.

7. Bake in the oven for 18–20 minutes, or until well risen, golden and firm to the touch. Spoon the reserved orange caramel syrup over the hot muffins. Cool in the tin for 10 minutes, then turn out onto a wire rack.

SPICED CARROT
Muffins with Soft Cheese

These muffins are really mini carrot cakes – perfect for lunchboxes and afternoon tea.

MAKES **12**

300g plain flour
225g caster sugar
2 teaspoons bicarbonate of soda
2 teaspoons ground cinnamon
1 teaspoon salt
175ml vegetable oil
175ml milk
3 eggs, lightly beaten
100g peeled carrot, grated
120g walnuts, chopped
150g raisins

FOR THE TOPPING
85g cream cheese or full-fat soft
    cheese, softened
40g butter, softened
125g icing sugar, sifted
¹/₂ teaspoon vanilla extract

1. Preheat the oven to 180°C/350°F/Gas mark 4. Grease a 12-cup muffin tin or line the cups with paper muffin cases.

2. For the muffins, mix the flour, sugar, bicarbonate of soda, cinnamon and salt in a large bowl. In a separate bowl or jug, mix together the vegetable oil, milk and eggs. Add the wet ingredients all at once to the dry ingredients together with the grated carrot, walnuts and raisins. Mix briefly until just combined.

3. Spoon the batter into the muffin cups, dividing it evenly. Bake in the oven for 20–25 minutes, or until risen and golden. Cool in the tin for 10 minutes, then turn out onto a wire rack and leave to cool completely.

4. For the topping, beat together the cream cheese or soft cheese and butter in a bowl until light and fluffy. Beat in the icing sugar and vanilla extract until the topping is thick and spreadable. Spread a large tablespoonful of the topping mixture on top of each muffin before serving.

BANANA & HAZELNUT Muffins

To toast hazelnuts, or any other nuts for that matter, spread them in a single layer on a baking sheet and put into a fairly hot oven (about 200°C/400°F/Gas mark 6) for about 5 minutes, or until golden and fragrant (smaller nuts may take less time, while larger nuts may need a couple of minutes extra).

MAKES 12

300g self-raising flour
2 tablespoons soft light brown sugar
50g toasted hazelnuts, chopped
3 large very ripe bananas, peeled
3 tablespoons vegetable oil
2 eggs, lightly beaten
80ml natural yoghurt
2 tablespoons demerara sugar

1. Preheat the oven to 200°C/400°F/Gas mark 6. Grease a 12-cup muffin tin or line the cups with paper muffin cases.

2. Mix the flour, brown sugar and hazelnuts in a large bowl. In a separate bowl, mash the bananas until fairly smooth, then stir in the vegetable oil, eggs and yogurt. Add the wet ingredients all at once to the dry ingredients and mix briefly until just combined.

3. Spoon the batter into the prepared muffin cups, dividing it evenly, then sprinkle the tops with the demerara sugar.

4. Bake in the oven for about 20 minutes, or until risen and golden. Cool in the tin for 10 minutes, then turn out onto a wire rack. Serve warm or cold.

MUFFIN TIP
Pecans, walnuts or toasted almonds would also work well in this recipe instead of hazelnuts.

PEANUT BUTTER & BANANA Muffins

The combination of peanut butter and banana is a popular sandwich filling, used here to create these delicious muffins!

MAKES 12

225g plain flour
100g rolled oats
50g soft light brown sugar
1 tablespoon baking powder
½ teaspoon salt
100g crunchy peanut butter
225ml milk
1 tablespoon maple syrup
1 egg, lightly beaten
2 very ripe bananas, peeled and
    mashed
1 tablespoon granulated sugar
1 teaspoon ground cinnamon

1. Preheat the oven to 200°C/400°F/Gas mark 6. Grease a 12-cup muffin tin or line the cups with paper muffin cases.

2. Mix the flour and oats in a large bowl, then stir in the brown sugar. Add the baking powder and salt and stir to mix.

3. In a separate bowl or jug, mix together the peanut butter, milk, maple syrup, egg and mashed bananas until well blended. Add the wet ingredients all at once to the dry ingredients, mixing until just combined.

4. Spoon the batter into the prepared muffin cups, dividing it evenly. Mix together the granulated sugar and cinnamon, then sprinkle this mixture over the tops of the muffins. Bake in the oven for about 20 minutes, or until risen and golden. Cool in the tin for 10 minutes, then turn out onto a wire rack. Serve warm or cold.

CINNAMON SWIRL
Muffins

Nothing could be more enticing than to break open these warm fragrant muffins and discover ripples of cinnamon sugar.

MAKES 10

250g self-raising flour
1 teaspoon baking powder
Pinch of salt
110g caster sugar
1 egg, lightly beaten
225ml milk
85g butter, melted
FOR THE CINNAMON SUGAR
2 teaspoons ground cinnamon
75g soft light brown sugar

1. Preheat the oven to 190°C/375°F/Gas mark 5. Grease 10 cups of a 12-cup muffin tin or line 10 cups with paper muffin cases. For the cinnamon sugar, mix together the cinnamon and sugar in a small bowl. Set aside.

2. For the muffins, mix the flour, baking powder, salt and sugar in a large bowl. In a separate bowl or jug, mix together the egg, milk and melted butter. Add the wet ingredients all at once to the dry ingredients and mix briefly until just combined.

3. Put a tablespoonful of batter into each prepared muffin cup. Sprinkle each muffin with a heaped teaspoon of cinnamon sugar, then spoon some more batter and cinnamon sugar into the muffin cups. Finish with a layer of batter, dividing it evenly. Using a fine skewer or the tip of a sharp knife, swirl the mixture in each muffin cup to achieve a marbled effect.

4. Bake in the oven for 18–20 minutes, or until risen and golden. Cool in the tin for 10 minutes (the sugar mixture will remain really hot, so don't be tempted to try them sooner), then turn out onto a wire rack. Serve warm or cold.

CARDAMOM & ORANGE Muffins

Cardamom is a lovely warm aromatic spice that has a natural affinity with oranges. These muffins are scattered with amber sugar crystals, which add a caramel flavour and crunchy texture to the muffins.

MAKES 12

4 green cardamom pods
300g self-raising flour
1 teaspoon baking powder
150g caster sugar
1 egg, lightly beaten
225ml milk
Finely grated zest and juice of 1 large
   orange
75g butter, melted
2 tablespoons amber sugar crystals

MUFFIN TIP
Select smaller amber sugar crystals to scatter over the muffins, or if you prefer, use roughly crushed brown sugar cubes or demerara sugar instead.

1. Preheat the oven to 190°C/375°F/Gas mark 5. Grease a 12-cup muffin tin or line the cups with paper muffin cases.

2. Split open the cardamom pods and using a pestle and mortar, crush the black seeds from the cardamom pods to a powder. Using a fine sieve, sift them with the flour and baking powder into a large bowl, discarding any large bits of spice left in the sieve. Stir in the caster sugar.

3. In a separate bowl or jug, mix together the egg, milk, orange zest and juice and melted butter. Add the wet ingredients all at once to the dry ingredients and mix briefly until just combined.

4. Spoon the batter into the prepared muffin cups, dividing it evenly, then scatter the tops with amber sugar crystals. Bake in the oven for about 20 minutes, or until risen and firm to the touch. Cool in the tin for 5 minutes, then turn out onto a wire rack. Serve warm or cold.

SWEET POTATO Muffins
with Pecans & Cinnamon

The flavour of the sweet potato goes beautifully with the cinnamon, and the chopped pecan nuts add a welcome crunch to these tasty muffins.

MAKES 12

1 large orange-fleshed sweet potato
125g butter, softened
225g caster sugar
2 eggs, lightly beaten
300g plain flour
2 teaspoons baking powder
¼ teaspoon salt
1 teaspoon ground cinnamon
½ teaspoon freshly grated nutmeg
225ml milk
65g pecans, chopped

MUFFIN TIP
Walnuts would also work well in this recipe instead of pecans, if you like.

1. Preheat the oven to 200°C/400°F/Gas mark 6. Grease a 12-cup muffin tin or line the cups with paper muffin cases.

2. Prick the sweet potato several times with a fork and place it on a small baking sheet or a piece of foil. Bake in the oven for 45–60 minutes, or until tender. Remove from the oven and set aside until cool enough to handle.

3. When cool, cut the sweet potato in half and scoop out the flesh. Transfer the flesh to a small bowl and mash until smooth – you should have about 225g mashed potato flesh. Set aside.

4. Cream the butter and sugar together in a large bowl. Beat in the eggs and sweet potato flesh. In a separate bowl or jug, mix together the flour, baking powder, salt, cinnamon and nutmeg. Add the flour mixture to the butter mixture alternately with the milk, mixing briefly until just combined. Fold in the pecans.

5. Spoon the batter into the prepared muffin cups, dividing it evenly. Bake in the oven for 20–25 minutes, or until risen and golden. Cool in the tin for 10 minutes, then turn out onto a wire rack. Serve warm or cold.

HONEY & PISTACHIO Muffins

This recipe is inspired by baklava, the sweet and sticky Middle Eastern pastry flavoured with nuts and honey. Use a scented honey for the best results.

MAKES 12

300g plain flour
1 tablespoon baking powder
½ teaspoon salt
1 teaspoon ground cinnamon
Pinch of ground cloves
3 tablespoons chopped pistachio nuts
3 tablespoons chopped blanched
    almonds
100g soft light brown sugar
4 tablespoons clear honey
225ml milk
2 tablespoons vegetable oil
2 eggs, lightly beaten

1. Preheat the oven to 200°C/400°F/Gas mark 6. Grease a 12-cup muffin tin or line the cups with paper muffin cases.

2. Mix the flour, baking powder, salt, cinnamon and cloves in a large bowl. Stir in 2 tablespoons of the pistachio nuts, 2 tablespoons of the almonds and the sugar.

3. In a separate bowl or jug, mix together 2 tablespoons of the honey with the milk, vegetable oil and eggs. Add the wet ingredients all at once to the dry ingredients and mix briefly until just combined.

4. Spoon the batter into the prepared muffin cups, dividing it evenly, then sprinkle the tops with the remaining mixed chopped nuts.

5. Bake in the oven for 18–20 minutes, or until risen and golden. Drizzle the hot baked muffins with the remaining 2 tablespoons of honey. Cool in the tin for 10 minutes, then turn out onto a wire rack. These muffins are best eaten warm.

COFFEE WALNUT
Muffins

MAKES 12

125g walnut halves
150g butter
150g granulated sugar
3 egg whites
4 egg yolks
1 teaspoon vanilla extract
150g plain flour
1 teaspoon baking powder

FOR THE COFFEE ICING

1½ tablespoons milk
Small knob of butter
1 tablespoon instant coffee granules
200g icing sugar, sifted
1 teaspoon vanilla extract

1. Preheat the oven to 180°C/350°F/Gas mark 4. Grease a 12-cup muffin tin or line the cups with paper muffin cases.

2. Reserve 12 walnut halves for decoration, then finely chop the remainder in a blender or food processor, but do not allow them to become pasty.

3. Melt the butter and sugar in a heavy-based saucepan over a low heat. Gently bring the mixture to the boil and cook for 2 minutes, stirring constantly. Be careful not to brown or burn the mixture. Remove the pan from the heat and set aside to cool.

4. Whisk the egg whites in a clean bowl until stiff peaks form; set aside. Add the egg yolks to the cooled sugar-butter mixture, then stir in the chopped walnuts, vanilla extract, flour and baking powder. Gently fold in the whisked egg whites to make a soft, thick batter.

5. Spoon the batter into the prepared muffin cups, dividing evenly. Bake in the oven for 15–20 minutes, or until golden and firm to the touch. Cool in the tin for 10 minutes, then turn onto a wire rack to cool completely.

6. For the icing, heat the milk, butter and coffee granules in a small saucepan over a low heat, stirring until the butter is melted. Add the icing sugar and vanilla extract and stir until smooth and combined, adding a little more icing sugar if necessary to make a spreading consistency. Spread some icing on top of each muffin and top with a walnut half.

GINGER RHUBARB Muffins with Crème Anglaise

MAKES 10

300g self-raising flour
2 teaspoons ground ginger
$1/2$ teaspoon baking powder
$1/2$ teaspoon bicarbonate of soda
$1/4$ teaspoon salt
140g caster sugar
150g fresh rhubarb, finely chopped
1 egg, lightly beaten
150ml milk
150ml soured cream
4 tablespoons vegetable oil
1 tablespoon demerara sugar

FOR THE CRÈME ANGLAISE
300ml milk
1 vanilla pod, split lengthways
3 egg yolks
1 teaspoon cornflour
1 tablespoon caster sugar

1. Preheat the oven to 190°C/375°F/Gas mark 5. Grease 10 cups of a 12-cup muffin tin or line 10 cups with paper muffin cases. Start making the Crème Anglaise. Pour the milk into a heavy-based saucepan, add the vanilla pod and heat to boiling point. Turn off the heat and leave to infuse for about 15 minutes.

2. For the muffins, mix the flour, ginger, baking powder, bicarbonate of soda, salt and caster sugar in a large bowl. Stir in the rhubarb. In a separate bowl mix together the egg, milk, soured cream and vegetable oil. Add the wet ingredients to the dry ingredients and mix briefly until just combined.

3. Spoon the batter into the prepared muffin cups, then sprinkle with demerara sugar. Bake in the oven for 18–20 minutes, or until well risen and golden. Cool in the tin for 5 minutes, then turn onto a wire rack.

4. While the muffins are baking, finish the Crème Anglaise. Whisk the egg yolks, cornflour and sugar together in a bowl until pale and creamy. Remove the vanilla pod from the milk and scrape out the black seeds. Add the seeds to the egg mixture. Reheat the milk to boiling point, then slowly pour into the egg mixture, whisking all the time. Pour back into the pan.

5. Cook over a very low heat, stirring constantly for 10–15 minutes, or until the mixture thickens enough to coat the back of the spoon; do not allow the mixture to boil. Serve the muffins warm with the Crème Anglaise.

PEANUT BUTTER Muffins

For a pure, unadulterated peanut butter hit, try these mouth-watering muffins accompanied by a glass of cold milk.

MAKES **12**

300g plain flour
1½ teaspoons baking powder
½ teaspoon salt
4 tablespoons finely chopped
   unsalted, roasted peanuts
100g soft light brown sugar
200g smooth peanut butter
175ml milk
2 tablespoons vegetable oil
2 eggs, lightly beaten
1 tablespoon demerara sugar

1. Preheat the oven to 190°C/375°F/Gas mark 5. Grease a 12-cup muffin tin or line the cups with paper muffin cases.

2. Mix the flour, baking powder and salt in a large bowl. Stir in 2 tablespoons of the chopped peanuts and the brown sugar. Add the peanut butter and rub in until the mixture resembles coarse breadcrumbs.

3. In a separate bowl or jug, mix together the milk, vegetable oil and eggs. Add the wet ingredients all at once to the dry ingredients and mix briefly until just combined.

4. Spoon the batter into the prepared muffin cups, dividing it evenly. Combine the remaining chopped peanuts and demerara sugar, then sprinkle this mixture over the tops of the muffins.

5. Bake in the oven for 16–18 minutes, or until risen and golden. Cool in the tin for 10 minutes, then turn out onto a wire rack.
Serve warm or cold.

BUTTER TART Muffins with Raisins & Walnuts

These muffins are everything a butter tart should be – gooey and buttery. You can leave out the nuts and raisins, if you prefer.

MAKES 12

200g raisins
175g granulated sugar
125g butter
125ml milk
1 teaspoon vanilla or rum extract
2 eggs, lightly beaten
300g plain flour
2 teaspoons baking powder
1 teaspoon bicarbonate of soda
Pinch of salt
65g walnuts, chopped
3–4 tablespoons golden syrup

MUFFIN TIP
Try using sultanas or chopped ready-to-eat dried apricots instead of raisins, and pecans or pine nuts instead of walnuts.

1. Preheat the oven to 190°C/375°F/Gas mark 5. Grease a 12-cup muffin tin or line the cups with paper muffin cases.

2. Combine the raisins, sugar, butter, milk and vanilla or rum extract in a saucepan. Cook over a medium heat, stirring almost constantly, until the mixture is hot and the sugar has melted. Bring just to a simmer, then remove the pan from the heat. Allow the mixture to cool for 10 minutes, then whisk in the eggs. Set aside to cool until just warm.

3. Mix the flour, baking powder, bicarbonate of soda and salt in a large bowl. Make a well in the centre and pour in the raisin mixture, stirring briefly until just combined. Gently fold in the walnuts, then spoon the batter into the prepared muffin cups, dividing it evenly. Bake in the oven for 15–17 minutes, or until risen and golden.

4. Remove from the oven and immediately drizzle about 1 teaspoon of golden syrup over the top of each muffin. Cool in the tin for 10 minutes, then turn out onto a wire rack. Serve warm or cold.

STICKY GINGERBREAD Muffins

These tasty muffins make a delicious dessert if served warm with creamy custard. Alternatively, eat them when cold, split and spread with a little butter.

MAKES 10

250g self-raising flour
1/2 teaspoon bicarbonate of soda
1/2 teaspoon salt
2 teaspoons ground ginger
1 teaspoon ground cinnamon
Pinch of freshly grated nutmeg
150g soft light brown sugar
2 tablespoons golden syrup
1 tablespoon molasses or
   black treacle
85g butter, cut into small pieces
175ml milk
1 egg, lightly beaten

1. Preheat the oven to 190°C/375°F/Gas mark 5. Grease 10 cups of a 12-cup muffin tin or line 10 cups with paper muffin cases.

2. Mix the flour, bicarbonate of soda, salt, ginger, cinnamon, nutmeg and sugar in a large bowl.

3. Put the golden syrup, molasses or black treacle, butter and about one-third of the milk in a small saucepan. Heat gently until the butter has melted. Stir with a fork until the syrup and molasses or treacle are blended, then stir in the rest of the milk, followed by the egg. Add the wet ingredients all at once to the dry ingredients and mix briefly until just combined.

4. Spoon the batter into the prepared muffin cups, dividing it evenly. Bake in the oven for about 20 minutes, or until well risen and firm to the touch. Cool in the tin for 10 minutes, then turn out onto a wire rack. Serve warm or cold.

MUFFIN TIP
To make measuring the syrup and molasses easier, wipe a little oil onto your measuring spoon. Alternatively, stand the jars in hot water for a few minutes to make the contents thinner and runnier.

CINNAMON & PECAN Muffins

If you can't find buttermilk, simply mix 1 teaspoon of white vinegar into 175ml milk and leave at room temperature for 1 hour until slightly curdled.

MAKES 12

300g plain flour
1 teaspoon baking powder
1 teaspoon bicarbonate of soda
Pinch of salt
125g butter, softened
175g caster sugar
2 eggs, lightly beaten
1 teaspoon vanilla extract
175ml buttermilk
75g soft light brown sugar
1 teaspoon ground cinnamon
65g pecans, coarsely chopped

1. Preheat the oven to 190°C/375°F/Gas mark 5. Grease a 12-cup muffin tin or line the cups with paper muffin cases.

2. Mix the flour, baking powder, bicarbonate of soda and salt in a large bowl. In a separate bowl, cream the butter and caster sugar together until light and fluffy. Gradually beat in the eggs and vanilla extract. Stir in the buttermilk.

3. Add the wet ingredients all at once to the dry ingredients and mix briefly until just combined. In a small bowl, mix together the brown sugar, cinnamon and pecans.

4. Spoon half of the batter into the prepared muffin cups, then sprinkle with half of the pecan and cinnamon mixture. Repeat with the remaining batter and pecan mixture, dividing it evenly and gently pressing the pecan mixture into the batter using the back of a spoon.

5. Bake in the oven for 20–25 minutes, or until well risen and firm to the touch. Cool in the tin for 10 minutes, then turn out onto a wire rack. Serve warm or cold.

SUGAR & SPICE
Muffins

Sometimes the simplest muffins are the best. These buttery spiced muffins fill the kitchen with a wonderful aroma as they bake.

MAKES 10

250g self-raising flour
1 teaspoon baking powder
1 teaspoon ground ginger
1 teaspoon ground cinnamon
¼ teaspoon freshly grated nutmeg
Pinch of ground cloves (optional)
Pinch of salt
150g caster sugar
1 egg, lightly beaten
150ml milk
75g butter, melted

FOR THE TOPPING
2 tablespoons soft light brown sugar
1 teaspoon ground cinnamon

1. Preheat the oven to 190°C/375°F/Gas mark 5. Grease 10 cups of a 12-cup muffin tin or line 10 cups with paper muffin cases.

2. For the muffins, mix the flour, baking powder, ginger, cinnamon, nutmeg, cloves, salt and sugar in a large bowl. In a separate bowl or jug, mix together the egg, milk and melted butter. Add the wet ingredients all at once to the dry ingredients and mix briefly until just combined.

3. Spoon the batter into the prepared muffin cups, dividing it evenly. Mix together the topping ingredients, then sprinkle this mixture over the tops of the muffins. Bake in the oven for 18–20 minutes, or until well risen and golden. Cool in the tin for 5 minutes, then turn out onto a wire rack. Serve warm or cold.

MUFFIN TIP
Ground mixed spice, or 'apple pie' spice, may be used instead of the combination of spices, if you prefer.

BUTTERED BRAZIL NUT Muffins

Lightly toasting the Brazil nuts in a little butter brings out their unique flavour, making them ideal for these tasty muffins.

MAKES 12

150g Brazil nuts, roughly chopped
75g butter
Pinch of freshly grated nutmeg
300g self-raising flour
1 teaspoon baking powder
$\frac{1}{2}$ teaspoon bicarbonate of soda
$\frac{1}{4}$ teaspoon salt
100g caster sugar
1 egg, lightly beaten
225ml milk
Few drops of almond extract

MUFFIN TIP
Check the muffins after 15 minutes baking time to make sure that the nuts aren't over-browning. If they are sufficiently coloured, cover the muffins with a piece of foil for the remaining cooking time.

1. Preheat the oven to 190°C/375°F/Gas mark 5. Grease a 12-cup muffin tin or line the cups with paper muffin cases.

2. Set aside 50g of the Brazil nuts. Melt 25g of the butter in a small non-stick frying pan. Add the remaining chopped Brazil nuts and cook over a low heat for a few minutes until just beginning to turn golden. Remove the pan from the heat, cool for 1 minute, then add the remaining butter and the nutmeg to the pan. Stir until melted, then set aside.

3. Mix the flour, baking powder, bicarbonate of soda, salt and sugar in a large bowl. In a separate bowl or jug, mix together the egg, milk and almond extract. Stir in the toasted Brazil nuts and melted butter mixture. Add the wet ingredients all at once to the dry ingredients and mix briefly until just combined.

4. Spoon the batter into the prepared muffin cups, dividing it evenly, then sprinkle the tops with the reserved Brazil nuts. Bake in the oven for about 20 minutes, or until well risen and firm to the touch. Cool in the tin for 5 minutes, then turn out onto a wire rack. Serve warm or cold.

COCONUT CRUMBLE & RASPBERRY Muffins

A crunchy coconut topping and smooth, tangy raspberry centre makes a tasty contrast in these tempting muffins.

MAKES 12

375g plain flour
1 tablespoon baking powder
100g desiccated coconut
225g caster sugar
2 teaspoons finely grated lime zest
2 eggs, lightly beaten
175ml milk
50ml coconut milk
85g butter, melted
4 tablespoons seedless raspberry jam

FOR THE COCONUT CRUMBLE TOPPING

40g plain flour
25g flaked coconut
1 tablespoon caster sugar
25g butter, cut into small pieces

1. Preheat the oven to 190°C/375°F/Gas mark 5. Grease a 12-cup non-stick muffin tin.

2. For the coconut crumble topping, place all the ingredients in a small bowl and rub in the butter until the mixture resembles coarse breadcrumbs. Set aside.

3. For the muffins, mix the flour, baking powder, desiccated coconut, sugar and lime zest in a large bowl. In a separate bowl or jug, mix together the eggs, milk, coconut milk and melted butter. Add the wet ingredients all at once to the dry ingredients and mix briefly until just combined.

4. Spoon about half of the batter into the prepared muffin cups. Make a small hollow in each and fill with 1 teaspoon of jam. Top with the remaining batter, dividing it evenly. Sprinkle the tops with the coconut crumble topping.

5. Bake in the oven for 20 minutes, or until well risen and golden. Cool in the tin for 10 minutes, then turn out onto a wire rack. Serve warm or cold.

MAPLE PECAN Muffins

These are made by first creaming the butter and sugar together, which gives the muffins a lighter and more spongy texture.

MAKES 12

125g butter, softened
150g caster sugar
2 tablespoons ground almonds
2 eggs, lightly beaten
65g pecans, coarsely chopped
300g plain flour
1½ teaspoons baking powder
2 teaspoons bicarbonate of soda
Pinch of salt
175ml buttermilk
7 tablespoons maple syrup
6–12 pecan halves, to decorate

1. Preheat the oven to 190°C/375°F/Gas mark 5. Grease a 12-cup muffin tin or line the cups with paper muffin cases.

2. Cream the butter and sugar together in a bowl until light and fluffy. Stir in the ground almonds, then gradually beat in the eggs. Stir in the chopped pecans.

3. Sift the flour, baking powder, bicarbonate of soda and salt over the creamed mixture. In a small bowl, blend the buttermilk with 4 tablespoons of the maple syrup. Pour the buttermilk mixture all at once over the flour and creamed mixture and mix briefly until just combined.

4. Spoon the batter into the prepared muffin cups, dividing it evenly, then top each muffin with a pecan half. Bake in the oven for about 20 minutes, or until well risen and firm to the touch.

5. Cool in the tin for 5 minutes, then turn out onto a wire rack. Brush or drizzle the remaining 3 tablespoons of maple syrup over the hot baked muffins and serve warm or cold.

MUFFIN TIP
Use real maple syrup for these muffins rather than synthetic maple-flavoured syrup.

PEAR & GINGER Muffins

If you prefer classic gingerbread muffins, leave the pears and pecans
out of the muffin batter mixture.

MAKES 12

125g white vegetable margarine,
 softened
125g caster sugar
50g molasses or black treacle
2 eggs, lightly beaten
1 teaspoon bicarbonate of soda
175ml buttermilk
300g plain flour
2 teaspoons ground ginger
$1/2$ teaspoon ground cinnamon
$1/2$ teaspoon ground cloves
65g pecans, chopped
2 ripe pears, peeled, cored and finely
 chopped

MUFFIN TIP
*Use 2 eating apples
instead of the pears to
ring the changes for
this recipe.*

1. Preheat the oven to 180°C/350°F/Gas mark 4. Grease a 12-cup muffin tin or line the cups with paper muffin cases.

2. Cream the margarine and sugar together in a bowl until light and fluffy. Stir in the molasses or black treacle. Beat in the eggs one at a time, beating well after each addition.

3. In a separate small bowl or jug, gently stir the bicarbonate of soda into the buttermilk until it has dissolved.

4. In a separate medium bowl, mix the flour with the ginger, cinnamon and cloves, then add the flour mixture to the creamed mixture alternately with the buttermilk. Fold in the pecans and pears.

5. Spoon the batter into the prepared muffin cups, dividing it evenly. Bake in the oven for about 20 minutes, or until risen and firm to the touch. Cool in the tin for 10 minutes, then turn out onto a wire rack. Serve warm or cold.

PUMPKIN, MAPLE SYRUP & WALNUT Muffins

Pumpkin purée, maple syrup and walnuts combine well to create these delicious moist muffins, ideal for Halloween.

MAKES 12

300g plain flour
2 teaspoons baking powder
½ teaspoon bicarbonate of soda
1 teaspoon ground cinnamon
½ teaspoon freshly grated nutmeg
¼ teaspoon salt
150g soft light brown sugar
65g walnuts, chopped
2 eggs, lightly beaten
250g pumpkin purée (fresh or canned)
175ml evaporated milk
3 tablespoons vegetable oil
1 tablespoon maple syrup

FOR THE TOPPING
1 tablespoon soft light brown sugar
30g walnuts, chopped

FOR THE FILLING
75g cream cheese or full-fat soft cheese, softened
2 tablespoons soft light brown sugar
2 tablespoons maple syrup

1. Preheat the oven to 200°C/400°F/Gas mark 6. Grease a 12-cup muffin tin or line the cups with paper muffin cases.

2. For the filling, mix together the cream cheese or soft cheese, sugar and maple syrup in a bowl until smooth. Set aside.

3. For the muffins, mix the flour, baking powder, bicarbonate of soda, cinnamon, nutmeg and salt in a large bowl. Stir in the sugar and walnuts. In a separate bowl or jug, mix together the eggs, pumpkin puree, evaporated milk, vegetable oil and maple syrup.

4. Add the wet ingredients all at once to the dry ingredients and mix briefly until just combined. Add the soft cheese filling to the batter and swirl through the mixture with a knife until the batter looks marbled. For the topping, mix together the sugar and walnuts in a small bowl.

5. Spoon the batter into the prepared muffin cups, dividing it evenly, then sprinkle the tops with the topping mixture. Bake in the oven for about 20 minutes, or until risen and golden. Cool in the tin for 10 minutes, then turn out onto a wire rack. Serve warm or cold.

ROSEMARY & BAY-SCENTED Muffins

Here, the subtle fragrance of rosemary and bay leaves is complemented by a sweet orange glaze to create these lovely muffins.

MAKES 10

1 tender fresh rosemary sprig, about 10cm long
2 dried bay leaves
Small strip of pared orange rind
150ml milk
1 tablespoon cold water
250g self-raising flour
1 teaspoon baking powder
Pinch of salt
150g caster sugar
1 egg, lightly beaten
90g butter, melted

FOR THE ORANGE GLAZE & DECORATION

200g icing sugar
Finely grated zest of $\frac{1}{2}$ orange
About $1\frac{1}{2}$–2 tablespoons unsweetened orange juice
Tiny fresh rosemary sprigs, to decorate (optional)

1. For the muffins, rinse the rosemary and bay leaves in cold water, then put them in a small saucepan with the pared orange rind, milk and water. Slowly bring the mixture to the boil, then remove the pan from the heat, cover with a lid and leave to infuse and cool for 20 minutes. Discard the herbs and orange rind.

2. Preheat the oven to 190°C/375°F/Gas mark 5. Grease 10 cups of a 12-cup muffin tin or line 10 cups with paper muffin cases.

3. Mix the flour, baking powder, salt and sugar in a large bowl. Stir the egg and melted butter into the herb-infused milk. Add the milk mixture all at once to the dry ingredients and mix briefly until just combined.

4. Spoon the batter into the prepared muffin cups, dividing evenly. Bake in the oven for 18–20 minutes, or until well risen and golden. Cool in the tin for 5 minutes, then turn onto a wire rack to cool completely.

5. For the orange glaze, sift the icing sugar into a bowl. Add the orange zest, then stir in $1\frac{1}{2}$ tablespoons of orange juice, adding a little more if necessary to make a smooth, fairly thin icing or glaze. Spoon the glaze over the tops of the muffins and decorate with tiny rosemary sprig, if you like, before serving.

SAVOURY
MUFFINS

BACON & CREAMY CORN Muffins

These are a variation on the popular corn muffin. They're great for breakfast or for a light lunch, served with a little green salad on the side.

MAKES 12

225g rindless streaky bacon rashers
1 small onion, finely chopped
150g plain flour
170g cornmeal or instant polenta
2 tablespoons caster sugar
4 teaspoons baking powder
½ teaspoon salt
200g canned creamed sweetcorn
125ml milk
1 egg, lightly beaten

1. Preheat the oven to 200°C/400°F/Gas mark 6. Grease a 12-cup muffin tin or line the cups with paper muffin cases.

2. Cook the bacon in a large frying pan (or under a preheated grill) until crisp. Remove the bacon from the pan and drain well on kitchen paper. Add the onion to the same pan and sauté for about 5–7 minutes, or until soft and lightly golden. Remove the onion from the pan. Break or chop the bacon into small pieces and set aside with the onion. Reserve about 3 tablespoons of the bacon fat (or substitute vegetable oil).

3. Mix the flour, cornmeal or polenta, sugar, baking powder and salt in a bowl. In a separate bowl or jug, beat together the creamed sweetcorn, milk, egg and reserved bacon fat (or vegetable oil). Add the corn mixture to the flour mixture and mix briefly until just combined. Fold in the reserved bacon and onion.

4. Spoon the batter into the prepared muffin cups, dividing it evenly. Bake in the oven for about 20 minutes, or until golden. Cool in the tin for 5 minutes, then carefully turn out onto a wire rack. These muffins are best served warm from the oven.

CAJUN-SPICED CORN Muffins

These muffins smell wonderful as they are baking and are a great accompaniment to any Cajun-style stew or fish dish.

MAKES 12

170g cornmeal or instant polenta
150g plain flour
1 tablespoon caster sugar
1 tablespoon baking powder
1 teaspoon salt
$\frac{1}{2}$ teaspoon bicarbonate of soda
$\frac{1}{2}$ teaspoon Cajun seasoning
175ml buttermilk
2 eggs, lightly beaten
85g frozen sweetcorn kernels
2 spring onions, finely chopped
2 tablespoons vegetable oil
$\frac{1}{4}$ teaspoon Tabasco sauce
  (or to taste)

1. Preheat the oven to 200°C/400°F/Gas mark 6. Grease a 12-cup muffin tin or line the cups with paper muffin cases.

2. Mix the cornmeal or polenta, flour, sugar, baking powder, salt, bicarbonate of soda and Cajun seasoning in a large bowl.

3. In a separate bowl or jug, mix together the buttermilk, eggs, sweetcorn, spring onions, vegetable oil and Tabasco sauce. Add the wet ingredients all at once to the dry ingredients and mix briefly until just combined.

4. Spoon the batter into the prepared muffin cups, dividing it evenly. Bake in the oven for 18–20 minutes, or until well risen and golden. Cool in the tin for 5 minutes, then turn out onto a wire rack. Serve warm.

FRESH TOMATO & MIXED OLIVE Muffins

A crunchy crumb, Parmesan and poppy seed topping adds
the final touch to these delicious savoury muffins.

MAKES 12

300g plain flour
1 tablespoon baking powder
1 tablespoon caster sugar
25g fresh Parmesan cheese, finely
   grated
3 tablespoons chopped fresh basil
1 egg, lightly beaten
175ml milk
100g butter, melted
1 tablespoon olive oil
4 medium ripe tomatoes, skinned,
   seeded and chopped
50g pitted mixed black and green
   olives, roughly chopped
1 clove garlic, crushed
Salt and freshly ground black pepper,
   to taste

FOR THE TOPPING
40g fresh white breadcrumbs
25g fresh Parmesan cheese, finely
   grated
2 teaspoons poppy seeds

1. Preheat the oven to 200°C/400°F/Gas mark 6. Grease a 12-cup muffin tin or line the cups with paper muffin cases.

2. For the muffins, mix the flour, baking powder, sugar, Parmesan cheese and basil in a large bowl. In a separate bowl, mix together the egg, milk, melted butter, olive oil, tomatoes, olives, garlic and salt and pepper. Pour the tomato mixture into the dry ingredients and mix until just combined.

3. Spoon the batter into the prepared muffin cups, dividing it evenly. For the topping, stir together the breadcrumbs, Parmesan cheese and poppy seeds. Sprinkle this mixture over the tops of the muffins.

4. Bake in the oven for about 20 minutes, or until well risen and lightly browned. Cool in the tin for 5 minutes, then turn out onto a wire rack. Serve warm or cold.

MEDITERRANEAN Muffins

These savoury muffins would make a delicious light lunch served with a simple green salad.

MAKES 12

125g self-raising flour

75g cornmeal or instant polenta, plus extra for sprinkling

1 teaspoon baking powder

2 teaspoons caster sugar

$\frac{1}{4}$ teaspoon salt

50g fresh Parmesan cheese, finely grated

1 tablespoon chopped fresh herbs such as thyme, oregano or rosemary

25g fresh basil leaves, torn into small pieces

4 spring onions, thinly sliced

50g toasted pine nuts

2 eggs, lightly beaten

5 tablespoons olive oil

150ml milk

150ml natural yoghurt

1. Preheat the oven to 190°C/375°F/Gas mark 5. Grease a 12-cup muffin tin or line the cups with paper muffin cases.

2. Mix the flour, cornmeal or polenta, baking powder, sugar, salt, Parmesan cheese, herbs, spring onions and pine nuts in a large bowl. In a separate bowl or jug, mix together the eggs, olive oil, milk and yoghurt. Add the wet ingredients to the dry ingredients and mix until just combined.

3. Spoon the batter into the prepared muffin cups, dividing it evenly, then sprinkle the tops with a little cornmeal or polenta. Bake in the oven for about 20 minutes, or until well risen and firm to the touch. Cool in the tin for 5 minutes, then turn out onto a wire rack. Serve warm or cold.

MUFFIN TIP

If using fresh rosemary, choose young tender sprigs and use only the leaves stripped off the woody stem.

CHEESE & SUN-DRIED TOMATO Muffins

Sun-dried tomatoes have a wonderfully concentrated flavour and have a natural affinity with salty olives, pungent garlic and oregano.

MAKES 10

300g plain flour
1 tablespoon baking powder
1 tablespoon caster sugar
150g grated mozzarella or Cheddar cheese
5 tablespoons olive oil
2 eggs, lightly beaten
125ml milk
2 cloves garlic, crushed
75g sun-dried tomatoes (drained if in oil), chopped
50g pitted black olives, roughly chopped
2 teaspoons chopped fresh or 1 teaspoon dried oregano
Salt and freshly ground black pepper, to taste

1. Preheat the oven to 190°C/375°F/Gas mark 5. Grease 10 cups of a 12-cup muffin tin or line 10 cups with paper muffin cases.

2. Mix the flour, baking powder, sugar and mozzarella or Cheddar cheese in a large bowl. In a separate bowl or jug, mix together the olive oil, eggs and milk. Stir in the garlic, sun-dried tomatoes, olives, oregano and a little salt and some black pepper to taste. Add the wet ingredients to the dry ingredients and mix briefly until just combined.

3. Spoon the batter into the prepared muffin cups, dividing it evenly. Bake in the oven for about 20 minutes, or until well risen and firm to the touch. Cool in the tin for 5 minutes, then turn out onto a wire rack. Serve warm or cold.

MUFFIN TIP

If the sun-dried tomatoes aren't moist, soak them for about 10 minutes in the milk and oil mixture before adding to the dry ingredients.

CHEESY DOUBLE CORN Muffins

These tasty muffins are fabulous served with a hot bowl of spicy chilli con carne or fresh tomato soup.

MAKES 12

125g plain flour
170g cornmeal or instant polenta
1 teaspoon bicarbonate of soda
1 teaspoon baking powder
2 teaspoons salt
50g white vegetable margarine
75g Cheddar cheese, grated
2 eggs, lightly beaten
225ml milk
200g canned creamed sweetcorn

1. Preheat the oven to 200°C/400°F/gas mark 6. Grease a 12-cup muffin tin or line the cups with paper muffin cases.

2. Mix the flour, cornmeal or polenta, bicarbonate of soda, baking powder and salt in a large bowl. Rub in the margarine until the mixture resembles coarse breadcrumbs. Stir in the Cheddar cheese.

3. In a separate bowl or jug, mix together the eggs and milk. Add the egg mixture to the dry ingredients, together with the creamed sweetcorn and mix briefly until just combined.

4. Spoon the batter into the prepared muffin cups, dividing it evenly. Bake in the oven for 20–25 minutes, or until risen and golden. Cool in the tin for 10 minutes, then turn out onto a wire rack. These muffins are best served on the day they are baked, warm from the oven if possible.

MUFFIN TIP
Most muffins can be frozen for up to 3 months and will take about 30 minutes to thaw at room temperature or just a few seconds in the microwave.

PLANTAIN & HERB Muffins

Plantains can be eaten at every stage of ripeness but must be cooked. When green, their flavour and texture is akin to potato; when ripe (and black), they are more similar to the bananas they resemble, becoming sweet and soft.

MAKES 12

300g plain flour
1 tablespoon baking powder
1 teaspoon bicarbonate of soda
1 teaspoon salt
1 tablespoon chopped fresh thyme
  leaves
1 tablespoon snipped fresh chives
1 tablespoon chopped fresh parsley
1 clove garlic, crushed
175ml natural yoghurt
150ml milk
2 eggs, lightly beaten
2 tablespoons vegetable oil
1 tablespoon horseradish sauce
1 large green plantain, peeled and
  grated

1. Preheat the oven to 200°C/400°F/Gas mark 6. Grease a 12-cup muffin tin or line the cups with paper muffin cases.

2. Mix the flour, baking powder, bicarbonate of soda and salt in a large bowl. Add the thyme, chives, parsley and garlic and mix well.

3. In a separate bowl or jug, mix together the yoghurt, milk, eggs and vegetable oil. Add the wet ingredients all at once to the dry ingredients, together with the horseradish sauce and grated plantain, and mix briefly until just combined.

4. Spoon the batter into the prepared muffin cups, dividing it evenly. Bake in the oven for 20–25 minutes, or until risen and golden. Cool in the tin for 10 minutes, then turn out onto a wire rack. Serve warm or cold.

HOT CHILLI & SWEETCORN Muffins

These colourful spicy muffins would be excellent served with a Mexican-style soup.

MAKES 12

150g plain flour
150g cornmeal or instant polenta
40g caster sugar
1 tablespoon baking powder
$^1/_2$ teaspoon salt
1 egg, lightly beaten
25g butter, melted
2 tablespoons olive oil
175ml milk
1 small red pepper, seeded and
   chopped
1 fresh green chilli, seeded and finely
   chopped
225g can sweetcorn kernels, drained
$^1/_2$ teaspoon ground paprika

1. Preheat the oven to 200°C/400°F/Gas mark 6. Grease a 12-cup muffin tin or line the cups with paper muffin cases.

2. Mix the flour, cornmeal or polenta, sugar, baking powder and salt in a large bowl. In a separate bowl, mix together the egg, melted butter, olive oil, milk, red pepper, chilli and sweetcorn kernels. Pour the sweetcorn mixture into the dry ingredients and mix briefly until just combined.

3. Spoon the batter into the prepared muffin cups, dividing it evenly, then lightly dust the tops with paprika. Bake in the oven for about 20 minutes, or until well risen and lightly browned. Cool in the tin for 5 minutes, then turn out onto a wire rack. Serve warm or cold.

MUFFIN TIP
For even spicier muffins, add $^1/_2$ teaspoon hot chilli powder to the dry ingredients.

COTTAGE CHEESE & CHIVE Muffins

These savoury muffins would make a very nice light lunch, served with some soup and perhaps a side salad.

MAKES 12

300g self-raising flour
½ teaspoon baking powder
½ teaspoon bicarbonate of soda
½ teaspoon salt
50g butter, softened
50g soft light brown sugar
1 egg, lightly beaten
250g cottage cheese
50ml skimmed milk
3 tablespoons snipped fresh chives

1. Preheat the oven to 190°C/375°F/Gas mark 5. Grease a 12-cup muffin tin or line the cups with paper muffin cases.

2. Mix the flour, baking powder, bicarbonate of soda and salt in a large bowl. In a separate bowl, cream the butter and sugar together until light and fluffy. Beat in the egg. Add the cottage cheese and milk and stir until well mixed. Add the cottage cheese mixture to the dry ingredients, together with the chives, and mix briefly until just combined.

3. Spoon the batter into the prepared muffin cups, dividing it evenly. Bake in the oven for about 20 minutes, or until risen and golden. Cool in the tin for 10 minutes, then turn out onto a wire rack. Serve warm or cold.

MUFFIN TIP
You could try using flavoured cottage cheese for this recipe if you like, but make sure that the added ingredients do not change the consistency.

SAUSAGE & CHEESE Muffins

Use the best quality sausages you can afford, as they are the predominant flavour in these tasty muffins.

MAKES 12

225g good-quality pork sausagemeat
1 small onion, grated
300g plain flour
2 tablespoons caster sugar
1 tablespoon baking powder
$1/4$ teaspoon salt
175ml milk
1 large egg, lightly beaten
50g butter, melted
50g Cheddar cheese, grated

1. Preheat the oven to 190°C/375°F/Gas mark 5. Grease a 12-cup muffin tin or line the cups with paper muffin cases.

2. Cook the sausagemeat in a large frying pan over a high heat for 8–10 minutes, or until cooked through and golden, breaking up the sausagemeat with a wooden spoon as it cooks. Remove the sausagemeat from the pan and drain on kitchen paper, then set aside. Add the onion to the pan and sauté for 3–4 minutes, or until softened. Remove the onion to a plate and set aside.

3. Mix the flour, sugar, baking powder and salt in a large bowl. In a separate bowl or jug, mix together the milk, egg and melted butter. Add the egg mixture all at once to the dry ingredients, together with the Cheddar cheese, sausagemeat and onion. Mix briefly until just combined.

4. Spoon the batter into the prepared muffin cups, dividing it evenly. Bake in the oven for about 20 minutes, or until well risen and golden. Cool in the tin for 10 minutes, then turn out onto a wire rack. These muffins are best served warm.

BEER & ONION
Muffins

This unlikely combination works really well in these muffins — creating the perfect partner to an afternoon watching the football or your favourite film.

MAKES 12

300g plain flour
2 tablespoons caster sugar
1 tablespoon baking powder
1 teaspoon salt
½ teaspoon freshly ground black pepper
½ teaspoon garlic powder
225ml beer, allowed to go flat and at room temperature
125ml vegetable oil
1 egg, lightly beaten
1 small onion, grated
1 tablespoon chopped fresh thyme leaves

1. Preheat the oven to 200°C/400°F/Gas mark 6. Grease a 12-cup muffin tin or line the cups with paper muffin cases.

2. Mix the flour, sugar, baking powder, salt, pepper and garlic powder in a large bowl.

3. In a separate bowl or jug, whisk together the beer, vegetable oil, egg, onion and thyme. Add the wet ingredients all at once to the dry ingredients and mix briefly until just combined.

4. Spoon the batter into the prepared muffin cups, dividing it evenly. Bake in the oven for 20–25 minutes, or until risen and golden. Cool in the tin for 10 minutes, then turn out onto a wire rack. Serve warm.

MUFFIN TIP
Always bake muffins as soon as you've filled the tins, on the middle oven shelf or just a little higher. Close the oven door as quickly as possible to prevent heat being lost.

CHEESE & ONION Muffins

These are deeply savoury muffins that go really well with soups or stews.

MAKES 12

4 tablespoons vegetable oil
1 large onion, coarsely chopped
300g plain flour
75g mature Cheddar cheese, grated
1 tablespoon baking powder
1 teaspoon onion salt
225ml milk
2 large eggs, lightly beaten

1. Preheat the oven to 180°C/350°F/Gas mark 4. Grease a 12-cup muffin tin or line the cups with paper muffin cases.

2. Heat 1 tablespoon of the vegetable oil in a frying pan, add the onion and sauté over a medium heat for 8–10 minutes, or until crisp and golden. Remove the onion from the pan and drain on kitchen paper, then set aside to cool.

3. Mix the flour, fried onion, Cheddar cheese, baking powder and onion salt in a large bowl. In a separate bowl or jug, mix together the milk, eggs and the remaining vegetable oil. Add the wet ingredients all at once to the dry ingredients and mix briefly until just combined.

4. Spoon the batter into the prepared muffin cups, dividing it evenly. Bake in the oven for 15–18 minutes, or until risen and golden. Cool in the tin for 10 minutes, then turn out onto a wire rack. Serve warm.

CRUMBLE-TOPPED BACON & CHEDDAR Muffins

These smoky bacon and cheese muffins have a tasty savoury crumble topping. They're best eaten while still warm.

MAKES 12

100g rindless smoked streaky bacon rashers
150g self-raising white flour
150g self-raising wholemeal flour
1 teaspoon caster sugar
1 teaspoon baking powder
½ teaspoon dry English mustard
100g Cheddar cheese, grated
4 tablespoons chopped fresh parsley
Freshly ground black pepper, to taste
1 egg, lightly beaten
275ml milk
75g butter, melted

FOR THE CRUMBLE TOPPING

25g butter
40g plain flour
25g Cheddar cheese, finely grated

1. Preheat the oven to 200°C/400°F/Gas mark 6. Grease a 12-cup non-stick muffin tin. For the crumble topping, rub the butter into the flour in a bowl until the mixture resembles fine breadcrumbs. Stir in the Cheddar cheese. Set aside.

2. For the muffins, fry the bacon in a non-stick frying pan until golden brown and crispy. Remove the bacon from the pan and drain on kitchen paper. Leave to cool, then break or chop the bacon into small pieces.

3. Mix the flours, sugar, baking powder and mustard in a large bowl. Stir in the Cheddar cheese, parsley, and bacon and season to taste with black pepper, to taste. In a separate bowl or jug, mix together the egg, milk and melted butter. Pour the wet ingredients into the dry ingredients and mix briefly until just combined.

4. Spoon the batter into the prepared muffin cups, dividing it evenly, then sprinkle the tops with the crumble mixture. Bake in the oven for about 20 minutes, or until well risen and lightly browned. Cool in the tin for 5 minutes, then turn out onto a wire rack. Serve warm or cold.

DOUBLE CHEESE & CHIVE Muffins

The mild onion taste of fresh chives enhances the flavour of the cheeses in these savoury muffins.

MAKES 12

300g plain flour
1 tablespoon baking powder
1 tablespoon caster sugar
¼ teaspoon salt
75g butter
50g fresh Parmesan cheese, finely grated
75g Red Leicester cheese, cut into tiny cubes
2 tablespoons snipped fresh chives
1 egg, lightly beaten
225ml milk

MUFFIN TIP
Scatter the cheese cubes in the middle and not towards the edges of the muffins, as they may over-brown and stick to the tin.

1. Preheat the oven to 190°C/375°F/Gas mark 5. Grease a 12-cup non-stick muffin tin.

2. Put the flour, baking powder, sugar and salt in a large bowl. Cut the butter into small pieces and rub into the flour mixture until the mixture resembles fine breadcrumbs. Reserve 2 tablespoons of the Parmesan cheese and 25g of the Red Leicester cheese. Stir the rest of each type of cheese into the flour mixture, together with the chives.

3. In a separate bowl or jug, mix together the egg and milk. Add the egg mixture all at once to the dry ingredients and mix until just combined.

4. Spoon the batter into the prepared muffin cups, dividing it evenly, then sprinkle the tops with the reserved Red Leicester cheese cubes. Scatter a little of the remaining Parmesan cheese on top of each muffin. Bake in the oven for 18–20 minutes, or until risen and golden. Cool in the tin for 10 minutes, then turn out onto a wire rack. Serve warm or cold.

PUMPKIN & CHEESE
Muffins

Crunchy and cheesy, these delicious muffins are perfect for a buffet or light lunch.

MAKES 12

300g plain flour
1 tablespoon baking powder
1 teaspoon bicarbonate of soda
1 teaspoon salt
100g firm goat's cheese, coarsely diced
4 tablespoons toasted pumpkin seeds
200g pumpkin purée (fresh or canned)
175ml natural yoghurt
2 eggs, lightly beaten
2 tablespoons vegetable oil

1. Preheat the oven to 200°C/400°F/Gas mark 6. Grease a 12-cup muffin tin or line the cups with paper muffin cases.

2. Mix the flour, baking powder, bicarbonate of soda and salt in a large bowl. Stir in the goat's cheese. Coarsely chop 2 tablespoons of the pumpkin seeds and set aside the remainder. Stir the chopped pumpkin seeds into the flour mixture.

3. In a separate bowl or jug, whisk together the pumpkin purée, yoghurt, eggs and vegetable oil. Add the wet ingredients all at once to the dry ingredients and mix briefly until just combined.

4. Spoon the batter into the prepared muffin cups, dividing it evenly, then sprinkle the tops with the remaining pumpkin seeds. Bake in the oven for 20–25 minutes, or until risen and golden. Cool in the tin for 10 minutes, then turn out onto a wire rack. Serve warm.

SWEET POTATO, ROASTED CHILLI & FETA Muffins

MAKES 12

1 medium orange-fleshed sweet
   potato
1 fresh hot red chilli
300g plain flour
1 tablespoon baking powder
$\frac{1}{2}$ teaspoon salt
1 clove garlic, crushed
1 teaspoon cumin seeds, toasted and
   lightly crushed
1 tablespoon chopped fresh basil
2 eggs, lightly beaten
225ml milk
3 tablespoons olive oil, plus extra for
   brushing
75g feta cheese, crumbled

1. Preheat the oven to 200°C/400°F/Gas mark 6. Grease a 12-cup muffin tin or line the cups with paper muffin cases.

2. Prick the sweet potato several times with a fork and place it on a small baking sheet or a piece of foil. Bake in the oven for 30–45 minutes, or until tender. Remove from the oven and set aside until cool enough to handle. Once cool, scoop out and mash the flesh. Set aside.

3. Brush the chilli with a little olive oil and place under a preheated grill or over a naked flame, turning frequently, until it is scorched and blackened all over. Put the hot chilli into a small plastic food bag and leave until cool enough to handle. Peel the chilli, removing all the blackened skin, then slit the chilli open lengthways and remove the stem, seeds and membranes. Finely chop the chilli flesh. Set aside.

4. Mix the flour, baking powder and salt in a large bowl. Stir in the garlic, cumin and basil. In a separate bowl or jug, beat together the eggs, milk, olive oil and mashed sweet potato. Add the egg mixture all at once to the dry ingredients, together with the chopped chilli. Fold in the feta cheese, mixing until just combined.

5. Spoon the batter into the prepared muffin cups, dividing it evenly. Bake in the oven for 20–25 minutes, or until well risen and golden. Cool in the tin for 10 minutes, then turn out onto a wire rack. These muffins are best served warm.

PIZZA Muffins

Combining all the great flavours of a pizza, but more compact, these pizza muffins make a tasty snack, ideal for lunch or brunch.

MAKES 12

5 tablespoons olive oil
65g mushrooms, sliced
50g pepperoni, chopped
85g lean cooked ham, chopped
1 onion, grated
150g grated mozzarella cheese
75g sun-dried tomatoes (drained if in oil), chopped
1 tablespoon crushed garlic
2 teaspoons chopped fresh or 1 teaspoon dried oregano
1 tablespoon chopped fresh basil
2 eggs, lightly beaten
125ml milk
Salt and freshly ground black pepper, to taste
300g plain flour
1 tablespoon baking powder

1. Preheat the oven to 190°C/375°F/Gas mark 5. Grease a 12-cup muffin tin or line the cups with paper muffin cases.

2. Heat 1½ tablespoons of the olive oil in a large frying pan. Add the mushrooms and cook over a high heat for about 5 minutes, stirring frequently, until the mushrooms are golden and tender. Remove the pan from the heat and set aside to cool.

3. Mix the pepperoni, ham, onion, mozzarella cheese, sun-dried tomatoes, garlic, oregano, basil and cooled mushrooms in a bowl.

4. In a separate bowl or jug, mix together the eggs, milk and remaining olive oil, then add this to the pepperoni mixture. Season to taste with salt and pepper.

5. Mix the flour and baking powder in a separate large bowl. Add the pepperoni mixture and mix briefly until just combined.

6. Spoon the batter into the prepared muffin cups, dividing it evenly. Bake in the oven for 20–25 minutes, or until risen and golden. Cool in the tin for 10 minutes, then turn out onto a wire rack. These muffins are best served warm.

SMOKED BACON & BLUE CHEESE Muffins

It's very important to drain the bacon well after frying so that it remains crisp and tasty for these choice muffins.

MAKES 12

225g rindless smoked streaky bacon rashers
300g plain flour
1 tablespoon baking powder
$\frac{1}{2}$ teaspoon salt
80g caster sugar
1 egg, lightly beaten
5 tablespoons water
175ml milk
About 10 fresh basil leaves, finely chopped
75g blue cheese, crumbled
65g walnuts, chopped

1. Preheat the oven to 180°C/350°F/Gas mark 4. Grease a 12-cup muffin tin or line the cups with paper muffin cases.

2. Fry the bacon in a large frying pan until crisp. Remove the bacon from the pan and drain on kitchen paper. Set aside to cool. Reserve about 5 tablespoons of the bacon fat (or substitute vegetable oil). Break or chop the bacon into small pieces and set aside.

3. Mix the flour, baking powder, salt and sugar in a large bowl. In a separate bowl or jug, mix together the reserved bacon fat (or vegetable oil), egg, water and milk. Add the wet ingredients all at once to the dry ingredients, together with the bacon, basil, blue cheese and walnuts, and mix briefly until just combined.

4. Spoon the batter into the prepared muffin cups, dividing it evenly. Bake in the oven for 20–25 minutes, or until risen and golden. Cool in the tin for 10 minutes, then turn out onto a wire rack. Serve warm.

MINI SEEDED Muffins

These little savoury muffins are packed with crunchy seeds. If you like, toast the seeds for a few minutes in a non-stick frying pan before using, to bring out their nutty flavour.

MAKES 18

225g self-raising flour
40g cornmeal or instant polenta
1/2 teaspoon baking powder
1/2 teaspoon dried mixed herbs
40g sunflower seeds
20g pumpkin seeds
1 tablespoon sesame seeds, plus
    2 teaspoons
Salt and freshly ground black pepper,
    to taste
1 egg, lightly beaten
2 1/2 tablespoons olive oil
150ml milk

1. Preheat the oven to 190°C/375°F/Gas mark 5. Grease one 12-cup non-stick mini muffin tin and one 6-cup non-stick mini muffin tin, or grease 18 cups of a 24-cup non-stick mini muffin tin. Alternatively, line the cups with paper muffin cases.

2. Mix the flour, cornmeal or polenta, baking powder, dried herbs, sunflower seeds, pumpkin seeds and 1 tablespoon of sesame seeds in a large bowl. Season generously with salt and pepper. In a separate bowl or jug, mix together the egg, olive oil and milk. Add the wet ingredients to the dry ingredients and mix briefly until just combined.

3. Spoon the batter into the prepared muffin cups, dividing it evenly, then sprinkle the tops with the remaining 2 teaspoons of sesame seeds. Bake in the oven for about 10 minutes, or until well risen and golden brown. Cool in the tin for 5 minutes, then turn out onto a wire rack.

Serve warm or cold.

MUFFIN TIP
These mini muffins are delicious with added cheese. Stir 50g finely grated mature Cheddar cheese or 25g finely grated fresh Parmesan cheese into the dry ingredients.

HEALTHY & SPECIAL DIET
MUFFINS

CINNAMON-SPICED COURGETTE Muffins

Choose smaller, firm courgettes rather than larger specimens for these muffins, as they will be less watery and will give a better end result.

MAKES 12

300g plain wholemeal flour
100g soft light brown sugar
1½ tablespoons baking powder
½ teaspoon salt
1 teaspoon ground cinnamon
175ml milk
2 eggs, lightly beaten
3 tablespoons sunflower oil
3 tablespoons clear honey
120g courgettes (prepared weight), grated

1. Preheat the oven to 190°C/375°F/Gas mark 5. Grease a 12-cup muffin tin or line the cups with paper muffin cases.

2. Mix the flour, sugar, baking powder, salt and cinnamon in a large bowl.

3. In a separate bowl or jug, mix together the milk, eggs, sunflower oil, honey and courgettes. Add the wet ingredients all at once to the dry ingredients and mix briefly until just combined.

4. Spoon the batter into the prepared muffin cups, dividing it evenly. Bake in the oven for about 20 minutes, or until risen and lightly browned. Cool in the tin for 10 minutes, then turn out onto a wire rack. Serve warm.

MUFFIN TIP
If grated courgette seems quite watery, drain it on kitchen paper before adding it to the muffin mix.

SOURED CREAM & RAISIN Muffins

The batter for this classic muffin can be prepared ahead and kept in the refrigerator for up to two weeks, if you like. The recipe is also easily halved.

MAKES 36

225ml boiling water
5 teaspoons bicarbonate of soda
225g white vegetable margarine
450g caster sugar
2 eggs, lightly beaten
2 tablespoons molasses or black
    treacle
750g plain flour
300g toasted bran sticks, such as
    All-Bran cereal
100g bran flakes
300g raisins
1 tablespoon salt
900ml buttermilk

1. Preheat the oven to 200°C/400°F/Gas mark 6. Grease three 12-cup muffin tins (or however many muffin cups you wish to use, see recipe introduction) or line the cups with paper muffin cases.

2. Pour the boiling water over the bicarbonate of soda in a very large bowl. Stir until dissolved, then set aside to cool. In a separate bowl, cream the margarine and sugar together until light and fluffy, then gradually beat in the eggs. Stir in the molasses or black treacle. In another bowl, mix together the flour, toasted bran sticks, bran flakes, raisins and salt.

3. Add the buttermilk to the bicarbonate of soda mixture. Add about half of the wet and dry ingredients alternately to the creamed mixture, stirring briefly to mix. Add the remaining wet and dry ingredients, mixing briefly until just combined.

4. Spoon the batter into the prepared muffin cups, dividing it evenly. Bake in the oven for about 20 minutes, or until risen and firm to the touch. Cool in the tin for 10 minutes, then turn out onto a wire rack. Serve warm or cold, split and spread with a little sunflower margarine.

BUTTERMILK BRAN Muffins

Contrary to its name, buttermilk is a low-fat product, which adds a unique flavour and lightness to muffins. Use your favourite dried fruit in these; sultanas, cranberries, blueberries, chopped dates or apricots all work well.

MUFFIN TIP

The muffin batter will be fairly wet when spooned into the muffin cups, but the oat bran and dried fruit will soak up a lot of moisture as the muffins cook.

MAKES 12

225g plain flour
100g oat bran, or a mixture of oat bran and oat germ
1 tablespoon baking powder
$\frac{1}{2}$ teaspoon salt
150g light muscovado sugar
75g dried fruit, such as sultanas, cranberries or chopped (stoned) dates
1 egg, lightly beaten
225ml buttermilk
4 tablespoons milk or unsweetened orange, apple or other fruit juice
1 tablespoon clear honey or molasses
6 tablespoons sunflower oil

1. Preheat the oven to 190°C/375°F/Gas mark 5. Grease a 12-cup muffin tin or line the cups with paper muffin cases.

2. Mix the flour, oat bran, baking powder, salt, sugar and dried fruit in a large bowl. In a separate bowl or jug, mix together the egg, buttermilk, milk or fruit juice, honey or molasses and sunflower oil. Add the buttermilk mixture all at once to the dry ingredients and mix briefly until just combined.

3. Spoon the batter into the prepared muffin cups, dividing it evenly. Bake in the oven for 18–20 minutes, or until risen and firm to the touch. Cool in the tin for 5 minutes, then turn out onto a wire rack. Serve warm or cold.

NUTRITIONAL NOTE
Oat bran is a delicious source of soluble dietary fibre, which can help to reduce high blood cholesterol when eaten as part of a low fat diet.

HONEY & CINNAMON Muffins

These muffins are relatively low in both fat and sugar. They're delicious served split and spread with a fruity conserve or concentrated fruit purée.

MAKES 10

225g plain flour
50g medium oatmeal, plus extra for sprinkling
50g light muscovado sugar
2 teaspoons baking powder
½ teaspoon bicarbonate of soda
¼ teaspoon salt
2 teaspoons ground cinnamon
1 egg, lightly beaten
150ml skimmed milk
225ml natural yoghurt
50g butter, melted
4 tablespoons clear honey

1. Preheat the oven to 200°C/400°F/Gas mark 6. Grease 10 cups of a 12-cup muffin tin or line 10 cups with paper muffin cases.

2. Mix the flour, oatmeal, sugar, baking powder, bicarbonate of soda, salt and cinnamon in a large bowl. In a separate bowl or jug, mix together the egg, milk, yoghurt, melted butter and honey. Add the wet ingredients all at once to the dry ingredients and mix briefly until just combined.

3. Spoon the batter into the prepared muffin cups, dividing it evenly, then sprinkle the tops with a little oatmeal. Bake in the oven for 18–20 minutes, or until well risen and golden. Cool in the tin for 5 minutes, then turn out onto a wire rack. Serve warm or cold.

NUTRITIONAL NOTE
Honey has a more intense sweetness than sugar, so you need less of it.

MUFFIN TIP
Fresh fruit such as raspberries, blackberries or blueberries may be added to the mixture, if you like.

DATE BRAN Muffins

Make the batter for these muffins the day before you want to
bake them, as the batter needs to rest overnight.

MAKES 12

300g plain flour
1 teaspoon bicarbonate of soda
1 teaspoon ground cinnamon
125g caster sugar
80g wheat bran
120g stoned dried or fresh dates,
    finely chopped
125ml buttermilk
175ml milk
3 tablespoons sunflower oil
1 egg, lightly beaten

1. Mix the flour, bicarbonate of soda, cinnamon and sugar in a large bowl.
Add the wheat bran and dates and mix well.

2. In a separate small bowl, mix together the buttermilk, milk, sunflower
oil and egg. Add the egg mixture to the dry ingredients, mixing briefly
until just combined. Cover and refrigerate overnight.

3. The next day, preheat the oven to 200°C/400°F/Gas mark 6. Grease a
12-cup muffin tin or line the cups with paper muffin cases.

4. Remove the batter from the fridge and spoon it into the prepared
muffin cups, dividing it evenly. Bake in the oven for about 20 minutes, or
until risen and golden. Cool in the tin for 10 minutes, then turn out onto
a wire rack. Serve warm or cold.

GLUTEN-FREE PEANUT BUTTER, BANANA & CHOC-CHIP Muffins

MAKES 12

3 medium bananas
2 eggs, lightly beaten
100g light muscovado sugar
140g smooth peanut butter
100g plain or milk chocolate chips
225g white or brown rice flour
1½ teaspoons gluten-free
   baking powder
½ teaspoon bicarbonate of soda
75g butter, melted
125ml buttermilk

1. Preheat the oven to 180°C/350°F/Gas mark 4. Grease a 12-cup muffin tin or line the cups with paper muffin cases.

2. Peel, then mash the bananas until fairly smooth in a large bowl, using a potato masher or fork. Stir in the eggs, sugar and peanut butter until well mixed. Alternatively, put these ingredients in a blender or food processor and blend together until smooth.

3. Stir in the chocolate chips, then sift over the rice flour, baking powder and bicarbonate of soda. In a separate bowl or jug, mix together the melted butter and buttermilk. Pour the wet ingredients over the banana mixture and dry ingredients and mix briefly until just combined.

4. Spoon the batter into the prepared muffin cups, dividing it evenly. Bake in the oven for about 18–20 minutes, or until risen and golden. Cool in the tin for 10 minutes, then turn out onto a wire rack. Serve warm or cold.

MUFFIN TIP
Use really ripe bananas for these muffins as they add sweetness to the mixture and will mash more easily to a purée.

NUTRITIONAL NOTE
If you also need to avoid dairy products, substitute rice milk mixed with 1 teaspoon of lemon juice or white vinegar for buttermilk, use dairy-free fat spread instead of butter, and use dairy-free chocolate or carob chips.

APPLE, CHEESE & OAT Muffins

This unusual combination is positively delicious. Try serving these tasty and wholesome muffins for breakfast.

MAKES 12

225g oat bran
75g plain wholemeal flour
50g soft light brown sugar
1½ tablespoons baking powder
1 teaspoon ground cinnamon
½ teaspoon salt
125ml unsweetened apple juice
3 tablespoons skimmed milk
1 egg, lightly beaten
2 tablespoons sunflower oil
2 tablespoons clear honey
1 medium eating apple, peeled, cored and diced
75g Cheddar cheese, cut into small cubes
3 tablespoons rolled oats

1. Preheat the oven to 200°C/400°F/Gas mark 6. Grease a 12-cup muffin tin or line the cups with paper muffin cases.

2. Mix the oat bran, flour, sugar, baking powder, cinnamon and salt in a large bowl. In a separate bowl, mix together the apple juice, milk, egg, sunflower oil and honey. Add the wet ingredients to the dry ingredients, together with the diced apple and Cheddar cheese, and mix briefly until just combined.

3. Spoon the batter into the prepared muffin cups, dividing it evenly, then sprinkle the tops with the oats. Bake in the oven for about 20 minutes, or until risen and golden. Cool in the tin for 10 minutes, then turn out onto a wire rack. Serve warm or cold.

GLUTEN-FREE APPLE, DATE & WALNUT Muffins

MUFFIN TIP
Unlike in other muffin recipes, the flours and other fine dry ingredients are sifted here to ensure that they are well-mixed and aerated.

MAKES 12

250g white or brown rice flour
50g soya flour
25g cornflour
1 tablespoon gluten-free baking powder
$\frac{1}{2}$ teaspoon salt
1 teaspoon ground cinnamon
$\frac{1}{2}$ teaspoon ground mixed spice
125g golden caster sugar
75g stoned dried dates, chopped
35g walnuts, chopped
2 eggs, lightly beaten
175ml milk
6 tablespoons sunflower oil
2 medium eating apples, peeled, cored and finely chopped

FOR THE TOPPING

65g walnuts, chopped
2 tablespoons golden caster sugar

1. Preheat the oven to 190°C/375°F/Gas mark 5. Grease a 12-cup muffin tin or line the cups with paper muffin cases.

2. For the muffins, sift the rice flour and soya flour, cornflour, baking powder, salt, cinnamon and mixed spice into a large bowl. Stir in the sugar, dates and walnuts. In a separate bowl, mix together the eggs, milk, sunflower oil and apples. Add this apple mixture all at once to the dry ingredients and mix briefly until just combined.

3. Spoon the batter into the prepared muffin cups, dividing it evenly. Mix together the topping ingredients in a small bowl, then sprinkle this mixture over the tops of the muffins.

4. Bake in the oven for about 20 minutes, or until risen and firm to the touch. Cool in the tin for 5 minutes, then turn out onto a wire rack. Serve warm or cold.

NUTRITIONAL NOTE
Gluten is a protein found in wheat and rye and intolerance to this substance is a symptom of coeliac disease, an inflammatory condition of the gastrointestinal tract.

EGGLESS CHOCOLATE Muffins

These are such moist chocolatey muffins that no one will guess there's anything different about them.

MAKES 9

50g creamed coconut (in a solid block), roughly chopped
6 tablespoons sunflower oil
225g self-raising flour
25g unsweetened cocoa powder
1 teaspoon baking powder
Pinch of salt
110g soft light brown sugar
2 teaspoons icing sugar

1. Preheat the oven to 180°C/350°F/Gas mark 4. Grease 9 cups of a 12-cup muffin tin or line 9 cups with paper muffin cases.

2. Pour 300ml of boiling water into a jug, add the creamed coconut and stir until it dissolves. Stir in the sunflower oil, then set aside to cool.

3. Mix the flour, cocoa powder, baking powder, salt and brown sugar in a large bowl. Add the wet ingredients to the dry ingredients and stir briefly until just combined.

4. Spoon or ladle the batter into the prepared muffin cups, dividing it evenly. Bake in the oven for 15–18 minutes, or until well risen and firm to the touch. Cool in the tin for 5 minutes, then turn out onto a wire rack. Dust the tops of the muffins with sifted icing sugar. Serve warm or cold.

NUTRITIONAL NOTE
These muffins are suitable for those who have a food intolerance or allergy to eggs and for vegans.

MUFFIN TIP
Use creamed coconut in a solid block rather than canned creamed coconut for these muffins.

HAZELNUT MINI Muffins

These mini savoury muffins are delicious served with a simple soup.

MAKES 30

3 tablespoons groundnut oil
100g blanched hazelnuts, chopped
150g self-raising white flour
75g self-raising wholemeal flour
40g cornmeal or instant polenta
$\frac{1}{2}$ teaspoon baking powder
Salt and freshly ground black
　pepper, to taste
1 egg, lightly beaten
175ml milk

NUTRITIONAL NOTE
Hazelnuts are a rich source of vitamin E. As well as being a powerful antioxidant, this vitamin helps to keep the heart healthy by preventing the oxidation of LDL cholesterol.

1. Preheat the oven to 190°C/375°F/Gas mark 5. Grease two 12-cup non-stick mini muffin tins and one 6-cup non-stick mini muffin tin, or one 24-cup non-stick mini muffin tin and one 6-cup non-stick mini muffin tin.

2. Heat 1 tablespoon of the groundnut oil in a non-stick frying pan. Add half of the chopped hazelnuts and cook over a low heat for a few minutes until the nuts are just beginning to colour. Remove the pan from the heat and stir in the rest of the groundnut oil to stop the nuts from further cooking. Set aside.

3. Mix the flours, cornmeal or polenta, baking powder and salt and pepper in a large bowl. In a separate bowl or jug, mix together the egg and milk. Stir in the toasted hazelnuts and oil mixture. Add the wet ingredients to the dry ingredients and mix briefly until just combined.

4. Spoon the batter into the prepared muffin cups, dividing it evenly, then sprinkle the tops with the remaining hazelnuts, pressing them gently into the batter. Bake in the oven for 10–12 minutes, or until well risen and golden brown. Cool in the tins for 5 minutes, then turn out onto a wire rack. Serve warm or cold.

WHOLEMEAL BANANA & WALNUT Muffins

The wholemeal flour in this recipe really emphasises the nutty flavour of these delicious muffins.

MAKES 12

150g self-raising wholemeal flour
150g self-raising white flour
2 tablespoons soft light brown sugar
65g walnuts, chopped
3 large very ripe bananas, peeled
3 tablespoons sunflower oil
2 eggs, lightly beaten
5 tablespoons soured cream
2 tablespoons clear honey

1. Preheat the oven to 200°C/400°F/Gas mark 6. Grease a 12-cup muffin tin or line the cups with paper muffin cases.

2. Mix the flours, sugar and walnuts in a large bowl. In a separate bowl, mash the bananas until fairly smooth using a potato masher or fork, then stir in the sunflower oil, eggs, soured cream and honey.

3. Add the wet ingredients all at once to the dry ingredients and mix briefly until just combined. Spoon the batter into the prepared muffin cups, dividing it evenly.

4. Bake in the oven for about 20 minutes, or until risen and golden. Cool in the tin for 10 minutes, then turn out onto a wire rack. Serve warm or cold.

COTTAGE CHEESE & RAISIN Muffins

This unusual combination of savoury and sweet works really well and creates very moist muffins.

MAKES 12

300g plain flour
375g toasted bran sticks, such as
    All-Bran cereal
175g caster sugar
1 tablespoon baking powder
1/2 teaspoon bicarbonate of soda
1 teaspoon ground cinnamon
1 teaspoon finely grated orange zest
1/2 teaspoon salt
250g cottage cheese
225ml natural yoghurt
2 tablespoons clear honey
50g butter, melted
2 eggs, lightly beaten
100g peeled carrots, grated
75g raisins
FOR THE TOPPING
2 tablespoons granulated sugar
1 teaspoon ground cinnamon

1. Preheat the oven to 200°C/400°F/Gas mark 6. Grease a 12-cup muffin tin or line the cups with paper muffin cases.

2. Mix the flour, toasted bran sticks, sugar, baking powder, bicarbonate of soda, cinnamon, orange zest and salt in a large bowl.

3. In a separate bowl, mix together the cottage cheese, yoghurt, honey, melted butter and eggs. Add the wet ingredients to the dry ingredients and mix briefly until just combined. Fold in the carrots and raisins.

4. Spoon the batter into the prepared muffin cups, dividing it evenly. Combine the sugar and cinnamon for the topping, then sprinkle this mixture over the tops of the muffins. Bake in the oven for 20–25 minutes, or until risen and golden. Cool in the tin for 10 minutes, then turn out onto a wire rack. Serve warm or cold.

GLUTEN-FREE FRESH BLUEBERRY Muffins

Suitable for a gluten-free diet, these simple fruit muffins will soon become a perennial favourite.

MAKES 9

75g rice flour
75g soya or potato flour
110g caster sugar
$1/4$ teaspoon salt
2 teaspoons gluten-free
   baking powder
2 eggs, lightly beaten
125ml milk
2 tablespoons lemon juice
150g fresh blueberries

1. Preheat the oven to 180°C/350°F/Gas mark 4. Grease 9 cups of a 12-cup muffin tin or line 9 cups with paper muffin cases.

2. Mix the flours, sugar, salt and baking powder in a large bowl. In a separate bowl or jug, mix together the eggs, milk and lemon juice. Add the wet ingredients all at once to the dry ingredients, tip in the blueberries and mix briefly until just combined.

3. Spoon the batter into the prepared muffin cups, dividing it evenly. Bake in the oven for about 20 minutes, or until risen and golden. Cool in the tin for 5 minutes, then turn out onto a wire rack. Serve warm or cold.

NUTRITIONAL NOTE
Blueberries are a good source of vitamin C and beta-carotene, both powerful antioxidants.

MUFFIN TIP
Rice and soya flour have a heavier texture than wheat flour, but the acid from the lemon juice reacts with the baking powder to give these muffins a better rise.

OAT & CHERRY Muffins

These wholemeal muffins are given a slightly nutty texture with the addition of rolled oats. They're delicious for a mid-morning snack and will keep up energy levels until lunchtime.

MAKES 10

50g rolled oats
275ml milk
2 teaspoons vanilla extract
225g self-raising wholemeal flour
1 teaspoon baking powder
½ teaspoon salt
150g light muscovado sugar
75g dried sweetened cherries, chopped
1 egg, lightly beaten
6 tablespoons sunflower oil
40g icing sugar (preferably unrefined), sifted

1. Preheat the oven to 190°C/375°F/Gas mark 5. Grease 10 cups of a 12-cup muffin tin or line 10 cups with paper muffin cases.

2. Put the oats in a medium bowl and pour over the milk and vanilla extract. Stir briefly, then set aside to soak for 10 minutes.

3. Mix the flour, baking powder, salt and muscovado sugar in a large bowl. Add half the chopped cherries to the flour mixture. Stir the egg and sunflower oil into the oat mixture. Add the oat mixture to the dry ingredients and mix briefly until just combined.

4. Spoon the batter into the prepared muffin cups, dividing it evenly. Bake in the oven for about 20 minutes, or until well risen and firm to the touch. Cool in the tin for 5 minutes, then turn out onto a wire rack and leave to cool completely.

5. Blend the icing sugar with 2 teaspoons of warm water in a small bowl to make an almost transparent, thin, smooth icing. Stir in the remaining dried cherries. Spoon some of this icing on top of each muffin. Leave until the icing has set before serving.

NUTRITIONAL NOTE
Rolled oats are whole oat grains that have been husked and then rolled to flatten, so they contain all the nutrients of the whole grain.

MUFFIN TIP
The icing adds a decorative touch to these muffins, but you can serve them simply dusted with a little icing sugar (preferably unrefined), if you prefer.

HONEY OAT BRAN Muffins

These lightly spiced oat bran muffins create a tasty snack, ideal for breakfast on the go or to pop into lunchboxes.

MAKES 12

200g self-raising white flour
150g self-raising wholemeal flour
1/2 teaspoon ground mixed spice
5 tablespoons soft light brown sugar
1 tablespoon baking powder
60g oat bran
100g sultanas
6 tablespoons sunflower oil
3 tablespoons clear honey, plus about
    3 tablespoons to drizzle
2 eggs, lightly beaten
225ml milk

1. Preheat the oven to 200°C/400°F/Gas mark 6. Grease a 12-cup muffin tin or line the cups with paper muffin cases.

2. Mix the flours, mixed spice, sugar, baking powder and oat bran in a large bowl. Add the sultanas and mix well.

3. In a separate bowl or jug, mix together the sunflower oil, 3 tablespoons honey, the eggs and milk. Add the egg mixture to the dry ingredients and mix briefly until just combined.

4. Spoon the batter into the prepared muffin cups, dividing it evenly. Bake in the oven for 20–25 minutes, or until risen and golden. Drizzle about 1 teaspoon of honey over the top of each hot baked muffin. Cool in the tin for 10 minutes, then turn out onto a wire rack. Serve warm or cold.

MUFFIN TIP
Oat bran should be available in supermarkets alongside the rolled oats, but if you have any difficulty in finding it, try your local health food shop.

HIGH-FIBRE Muffins

Although these muffins are fairly low in fat and sugar, juices from the carrot and banana will ensure they stay beautifully moist and will help to sweeten them as well.

MAKES 12

150g self-raising white flour
110g self-raising wholemeal flour
2 teaspoons baking powder
½ teaspoon ground cinnamon
½ teaspoon ground ginger
50g light muscovado sugar
Pinch of salt
1 large ripe banana, peeled and
  roughly chopped
1 large carrot, coarsely grated
75g sultanas
50g hazelnuts, chopped
1 egg, lightly beaten
50g sunflower margarine, melted
225ml skimmed milk

1. Preheat the oven to 200°C/400°F/Gas mark 6. Grease a 12-cup muffin tin or line the cups with paper muffin cases.

2. Mix the flours, baking powder, cinnamon, ginger, sugar and salt in a large bowl. Stir in the banana, carrot, sultanas and hazelnuts. In a separate bowl or jug, mix together the egg, melted margarine and milk. Add the wet ingredients to the dry ingredients and mix until just combined.

3. Spoon the batter into the prepared muffin cups, dividing it evenly. Bake in the oven for about 20 minutes, or until well risen and firm to the touch. Cool in the tin for 10 minutes, then turn out onto a wire rack. Serve warm or cold.

NUTRITIONAL NOTE
Using sunflower margarine instead of butter adds flavour to the muffins and ensures that they are low in saturated fat too.

MUFFIN TIP
While most muffins should be eaten within a day of making (or frozen as soon as they are cool), moist muffins like these can be kept for up to three days in an airtight container in the fridge.

INDEX